GW01032996

für Paul Benn,
mit vermbest wilk,

from

Bernd Montgomery Rydel

22.VII.96.

War, Women, and Poetry, 1914–1945

War, Women, and Poetry, 1914–1945

British and German
Writers and Activists

Joan Montgomery Byles

DELAWARE

Newark: University of Delaware Press
London: Associated University Presses

Associated University Presses
440 Forsgate Drive
Cranbury, NJ 08512

Associated University Presses
25 Sicilian Avenue
London WC1A 2QH, England

Associated University Presses
P.O. Box 338, Port Credit
Mississauga, Ontario
Canada L5G 4L8

The paper used in this publication meets the requirements of the American National Standard for Permanence of Paper for Printed Library Materials Z39.48-1984.

Library of Congress Cataloging-in-Publication Data

Byles, Joan Montgomery, 1939–
    War, women, and poetry, 1914–1945 : British and German writers and activists / Joan Montgomery Byles.
        p. cm.
    Includes bibliographical references and index.
    ISBN 0-87413-563-X (alk. paper)
    1. War poetry, English—Women authors—History and criticism.
2. War poetry, English—Men authors—History and criticism.
3. English poetry—20th century—History and criticism. 4. World War, 1914–1918—Literature and the war. 5. World War, 1939–1945—Literature and the war. 6. Literature, Comparative—English and German. 7. Literature, Comparative—German and English. 8. World War, 1914–1918—Women—Great Britain. 9. World War, 1939–1945—Women—Great Britain. 10. World War, 1914–1918—Women—Germany. 11. World War, 1939–1945—Women—Germany. 12. Authorship—Sex differences. I. Title.
PR605.W65B95 1995
821'.9109358—dc20   94-48454
                                                                 CIP

To Peter, my closest reader
and
to Simon and Jonathan

Tout comprendre, c'est tout pardonner.
—Mme. de Staël

Contents

List of Abbreviations   9

Note on Mass-Observation   11

Acknowledgements   13

Introduction   17

1. Women's Experience of World War I: Britain and
   Germany   23

2. British Women Poets and Soldier Poets of
   World War I   42

3. Women between the World Wars, 1918–1939   74

4. Women's Experience of World War II: Britain and
   Germany   105

5. British Women and Men Poets of World War II   140

Conclusion   173

Notes   177

Works Cited   185

Index   192

Abbreviations

ARP	Air Raid Precautions
ATS	Auxiliary Territorial Service
BDF	Bund Deutscher Frauenvereine
BDM	Bund Deutscher Mädchen
BEF	British Expeditionary Force
HJ	Hitler Jugend
HMSO	His/Her Majesty's Stationery Office
ILP	Independent Labour Party
MP	Member of Parliament
NSDAP	Nationalsozialistische Deutsche Arbeiterpartei (the Nazi party)
NUWSS	National Union of Women's Suffrage Societies
SPD	Sozialdemokratische Partei Deutschlands
VAD	(Member of) Voluntary Aid Detachment
WAAC	Women's Army Auxiliary Corps
WAAF	Women's Auxiliary Air Force
WILPF	Women's International League for Peace and Freedom
WRNS	Women's Royal Naval Service
WSPU	Women's Social and Political Union
WVS	Women's Voluntary Service

Note on Mass-Observation

Mass-Observation was an organization established in 1937 in Britain to create what it termed "an anthropology of ourselves". It employed a team of observers to record social behavior and conversations, and also made use of questionnaires, interviews, surveys, and volunteer diarists. After 1949 it changed its character and became a limited company engaged in market research. A huge mass of material collected between 1937 and about 1949 is archived at the University of Sussex, which has resumed the collection of contemporary material. A brief history may be found in Sheridan, *Wartime Women: A Mass-Observation Anthology,* 4–5, 265–67.

Acknowledgments

When I think back over the last five or so years it has taken me to research and write this book, I want first of all to express my gratitude to my family for their forebearance during my absences from family life that work on the book demanded. I owe an enormous debt of gratitude to Peter Byles for his unfailing patience and help of the most invaluable kind.

I want also to express my appreciation of colleagues and friends whose active interest and encouragement in the composition of the book have been of very great assistance. I think especially of Edwin Bock, Jay Halio, Angela Moorjani, and Charlotte Zoe Walker. Conversations with Simon and Jonathan Byles have been an important and rewarding part of my writing.

I am also very much indebted to the staff of the British Library, The Fawcett Library, The Imperial War Museum Library, and Syracuse University Library, especially Eileen Derycke and Mary Walsh. My greatest debt is to David Doughan of the Fawcett Library.

Permission to reprint copyright material in this book is gratefully acknowledged. Apologies are offered to those copyright-holders whom it has proved impossible to locate.

Mabel Esther Allan: extract from "Immensity" from *Time to Go Back*, Abelard-Schuman Ltd., 1972. Reprinted by permission of the author.

Vera Bax: "To Richard, my son" from *The Distaff Muse*, ed. Bax and Stewart, Hollis & Carter Ltd., 1949; "To Billy, my son", and extract from "The Fallen" from *Anthology for Verse Speakers*, ed. E. Guy Pertwee, Samuel French Ltd., 1950. Reprinted by permission of Paul A. North, literary executor.

Frances Bellerby: extracts from "War Casualty in Europe" from *Plash Mill*, Peter Davies Ltd., 1946, reprinted by William Heinemann Ltd. Reprinted by permission of Reed Book Services.

Winifred Boileau: "Sounds". First published in *Poems of the Second World War: the Oasis Selection*, Dent/Everyman. Reprinted by kind permission of the Salamander Oasis Trust.

Vera Brittain: extract from "To My Brother" from *Verses of a VAD*, Erskine MacDonald, 1918. Extracts from *Seed of Chaos: What Mass Bombing Really Means*, published by The Bombing Restriction Committee, 1944. Reprinted by permission of Paul Berry, literary executor.

Margaret Postgate Cole: extracts from "Afterwards" from *Poems*, George Allen & Unwin Ltd., 1918. Reprinted by permission of Mr. H.J.D. Cole.

Marion Coleman, extracts from "Monte Cassino 1945" from *Myself Is All I Have*, Outposts Publications, 1969. Reprinted by permission of the poet's literary executor.

Leslie Coulson: extract from "Who Made the Law?" from *English Poetry of the First World War*, ed. J. H. Johnston, Princeton University Press, 1964. Reprinted by permission of Princeton University Press.

Eva Dobell: extracts from "Night Duty" and "Pluck" from *A Bunch of Cotswold Grasses*, Arthur H. Stockwell Ltd., 1919. Reprinted by permission of P.H.M. Dobell.

Keith Douglas: "Elegy for an 88 Gunner." Published in *Poems of the Second World War: The Oasis Selection*, Dent/Everyman. Reprinted by kind permission of the Salamander Oasis Trust.

Eleanor Farjeon: extract from "Peace" from *Sonnets and Poems*, B. H. Blackwell Ltd. 1918. Reprinted by permission of David Higham Associates Ltd.

Karen Gershon: "Home" and an extract from "A Jew's Calendar" from *Selected Poems*, Victor Gollancz Ltd., 1966. Reprinted by permission of the author.

Grace Griffiths: "Doodlebugs," published in *Poems of the Second World War: The Oasis Selection*, Dent/Everyman. Reprinted by kind permission of the Salamander Oasis Trust.

Pamela Holmes: "War Baby" and "Missing, Presumed Killed." Reprinted by permission of the author.

Tennyson F. Jesse: "Note to Isolationists 1940" from *The Compass*, 1951 (private circulation). Reprinted by permission of Joanna Colenbrander.

Cecilia Jones: Extract from "Shipbound." Published in *Poems of the Second World War: The Oasis Selection*, Dent/Everyman. Reprinted by kind permission of the Salamander Oasis Trust.

Patricia Ledward: extracts from "In Memoriam (Timothy Corsellis, killed flying)" from *Poems of This War by Younger Poets*, eds. P. Ledward and C. Strang, Cambridge University Press, 1942. Reprinted by permission of Cambridge University Press.

Alun Lewis: extracts from "Burma Casualty" and "The Mahratta Ghats" from *Ha! Ha! Among the Trumpets*, George Allen & Unwin Ltd., 1945. Reprinted by permission of Harper Collins.

Rose Macaulay: extracts from "The Shadow" and "Picnic" from *Three Days*, Constable & Co. Ltd. 1919. Reprinted by permission of Peters, Fraser & Dunlop Group Ltd.

Ethel Mannin: "The Song of the Bomber" from *Verse of Valour*, Art and Educational Publishers Ltd., 1943. Reprinted by permission of Jean Faulks, literary executor.

Wilfred Owen: extracts from "Miners" from *Collected Poems*, ed. C. Day Lewis, Chatto & Windus 1944, 1963, and from "Anthem for Doomed Youth," "Insensibility," "A Terre," "Strange Meeting," and "Dulce et Decorum Est" from The Poems of Wilfred Owen, ed. Edmund Blunden, Viking Press 1931. Reprinted by permission of the estates of the Editors and Random House.

Anne Ridler: extracts from "Now as Then" from *The Nine Bright Shiners*, Faber & Faber Ltd. 1943, and *Collected Poems*, Carcanet Press, Manchester, 1994. Reprinted by permission of the author.

Siegried Sassoon: extracts from "They," "Base Details," "Glory of Women," and "Suicide in the Trenches" from *Selected Poems*, William Heinemann Ltd., 1925, and from "Counter-Attack" from

Introduction

This book is about European, especially British and German women's experience of World War I and World War II. The focus is essentially on an examination of women's literature in relation to war, rather than on women and war in general. The book is also concerned with men's literary response, particularly the poetic. The study then is both literary and historical and seeks to interweave the historical circumstances of these two appalling wars with women's and men's literary response, particularly the poetic response. I take a humanist rather than a strictly feminist view of these issues. For while the book focuses on women's all-round experience of war, it is also very much concerned with British men's creative poetic response to war. By addressing aspects of both the British poetic and the German and British prose documentary responses it is hoped that a more representative and balanced view will be achieved.

The book asks what the impact of each war was upon women's lives, and it focuses on how women writers represented that impact in their writing, particularly in their poetry of the two world wars. I also look at these women between the two wars, particularly their political experience and the threat that fascism represented to all women, but most of all to German women. I ask how living through this period changed women's social and political awareness of peace and war, how the wars changed women's image of themselves, and how women protested or supported the two wars.

The approach to social history is not that which would be taken by a social historian; rather it is a literary approach to social history. Furthermore, it is one that looks at social history as poets and writers would, using imagination as the vehicle of understanding and representation. In other words, the methodology as a whole seeks to show how literature, and poetry in particular, articulates perspectives on the historical, social, and cultural realities of war. One definition of war poetry might be a body of work whose content has been shaped and intensified by war experiences. However, these experiences are not just social-historical incidents in a poetic text; they are representations and responses to the terrifying impact of war on these women and men who are also poets. I shall be looking primarily, then, at how the historical-social situation of war manifests itself in artistic expression, but also of necessity at the actual historical-social events themselves. This war literature demonstrates the poets' concern with the historic fate of individuals at war, and with the human cost of war.

Once World War I was over and women were granted the vote, in Britain in December 1917 and in Germany in November 1918, what did these women do with this new power they had achieved? How many women became politicians? Did women vote for women? What were the obstacles women politicians had to overcome? What did the antiwar groups such as the British and German associations of the Women's International League for Peace and Freedom do in the twenties and thirties? In 1939 there was no acceptable way for British women to be antiwar and antifascist. Some of them renounced their pacifism while others, such as Vera Brittain, remained steadfastly antiwar.

Once World War II was declared, women were very much more involved in every way than in World War I. How did their experiences differ from those of women during World War I? How were they the same? In December 1941 there was, for example, general conscription of women for the first time in British history. In many ways the home front was just as dangerous and terrifying a place to be as the front line. How did women in London and Berlin react to the blitz of their cities? Vera Brittain's account of "precision bombing" is compared with two eyewitness accounts of the Berlin raids, those of Christabel Bielenberg and Marie Vassiltchikov.

Women writers are important recorders of women's historical experience, and they give us invaluable insight into women's lives and their reactions and feelings in these momentous times. Some of the following writers, both women and men, are among the most representative. In chapter 1 they are: Emmeline Pankhurst and her two daughters, Christabel and Sylvia, Emily Hobhouse, Helena Swanwick, and Millicent Fawcett. Chapter 2 explores women's poetry of World War I and includes such poets as Rose Macaulay, Charlotte Mew, Alice Meynell, Edith Sitwell, and May Sinclair, and the soldier-poets Wilfred Owen, Siegfried Sassoon, and Edmund Blunden. The women writers of chapter 3 are mostly journalists writing in the women's newspapers of the late 1930s. Chapter 4 looks at German and British women prose documentary writers who witnessed the blitz of London and Berlin: Christabel Bielenberg, the White Russian emigrée Marie Vassiltchikov, and Vera Brittain. Chapter 4 also cites some of the nonfiction work of Virginia Woolf and the fictionalized autobiography of the German writer, Christa Wolf. Chapter 5 considers women's and men's poetry of World War II concentrating on such poets as Frances Bellerby, Vera Bax, Patricia Ledward, Anne Ridler, and Sylvia Townsend Warner as well as Sydney Keyes, Alun Lewis, and Keith Douglas.

For many poets, both women and men, the war was less a social-political situation than one of horror, suffering, and death. The mood of the poetry seeks the truth underlying women's and men's experience of war. Most of the poems attempt to address the profound moral problems posed by this most terrible of human activities. In comparing the war poetry of men and women we can see important differences and important similarities that together offer us a comprehensive view of the effect of war upon the minds and senses of women and men. Both views are necessary for our understanding of the mortal significance of war in the lives of women and men.

War, Women, and Poetry,
1914–1945

1

Women's Experience of World War I: Britain and Germany

The Woman Suffrage campaign, and the militant Suffragettes in particular, shocked Edwardian England and contributed markedly to the social unrest which many observers saw as one of the outstanding features of the years after 1900. The Suffragist movement, begun in 1867, was given immense impetus by the militant suffragists who forced the movement forward. Their militant tactics between 1900 and 1914 did much to rouse public attention to women's suffrage. At the same time many suffragists lamented that clamor and hysterics were news, whereas reasoned argument was not. However, the militants certainly brought a sense of urgency to the movement. As Lord Baldwin said when unveiling the statue of Emmeline Pankhurst outside the Houses of Parliament on 6 March 1930, "If Mrs. Pankhurst did not make the movement, it was she who set the heather on fire" (Fulford 1957, 238).

Changed Social Conditions of Women, 1903–1918

There was a steady mobilization of women after 1903, not just for the vote, but for much greater educational and, later, job opportunities. By 1911 about 29 percent of the work force was female and most workers were working-class. Apart from the cotton industry the largest source of employment of working-class women was domestic service. All women suffered from the assumption that they could not work after marriage (Braybon and Summerfield 1987, 11–19).

At this time women were also striving for much greater individual freedom. Acquiring the important knowledge of birth control methods meant many middle-class women were less burdened by large numbers of children; but, many working-class women complained of the difficulty of obtaining contraceptive advice. Of course the churches' view of married sex was that it was for procreation only, certainly not for the woman's pleasure. Yet another important and related change in women's perception of themselves came from the field of biology. Biological research destroyed two widespread if contradictory beliefs, namely that women provided merely an environment for a male-produced embryo and, secondly, that the female determined the sex of children. What was happening was a slow but profound change in women's self-image.

As several commentators have pointed out, the government's persistent opposition to the women's cause made the mobilization of women more urgent and drastic, and this, too, was part of the process of changing their image of themselves.[1] Both processes were speeded up by women's experience during the period 1914–18.

World War I provided all classes of women with important opportunities to work outside the home.[2] The impressive achievements of women doctors and nurses, of women police and other service auxiliaries, of former domestic servants in factories, eventually had an enormous influence on public opinion in favor of women's suffrage.

As editor of *The Suffragette*, Christabel Pankhurst was well aware of the importance of suffragettes being in charge of their own image. In the 30 January 1914 issue she wrote:

> The WSPU [Women's Social and Political Union] must not only be strong; it must not only be independent; it must not only be uncompromising. It must also APPEAR to be strong, it must APPEAR to be independent, it must APPEAR to be uncompromising. (Christabel Pankhurst, "The Inner Policy of the WSPU." *The Suffragette* 30 January 1914, 2 [68]: 353).[3]

Her mother, Emmeline Pankhurst, believed that once a suffragist became militant she won a freedom and strength of spirit:

> It is right for (women) to be fierce as well as mild, to be strong as well as gentle. While they are mild and gentle towards their friends, they must be fierce and strong before their enemies and all who despitefully use them. (Christabel Pankhurst, 10 January 1913. "Militancy a Virtue." *The Suffragette* 1 [13]: 186, quoted in Sarah, *Feminist Theorists*, 280)

It is not difficult to understand how this kind of militancy became nationalist militarism. The fight for the vote was subsumed by the fight for king and country. In other words, the prowar suffragists transferred their militant tactics from winning emancipation to winning the war. According to Rover, during the war Christabel and Emmeline Pankhurst "expressed an almost jingoistic patriotism." Indeed, writing of Emmeline Pankhurst's enthusiasms, Rover states that during the war she "practically lost interest in women's suffrage, devoting herself to patriotic causes" (Rover 1967, 75).

Writing of the possibility of a Speaker's Conference in the autumn of 1916 as the best way to ensure the franchise question, Harrison says: "Mrs. Pankhurst did not help matters at this crucial stage by authorising Commander Bellairs on 16 August 1916 to voice the WSPU's view in the House of Commons that servicemen should get the vote whether women received it or not." Bellairs went on to explain to the Members of Parliament that the WSPU "will not allow themselves to be used to prevent soldiers and sailors from being given the vote" (Harrison 1978, 209).[4] However, over forty suffrage societies remained actively working for women's emancipation during the war.

The Split between the Pro- and Antiwar Suffragists, 1914–1918

The picture is a complex one; Emmeline Pankhurst and her younger daughter Christabel identified their movement with the war effort—indeed their prewar activism became aggressive nationalism. The idea of militarism as a yet more emphatic form of patriarchy did not seem to occur to them. Millicent Fawcett, the chairwoman of the other main suffrage society, the National Union of Women's Suffrage Societies (NUWSS), who believed in the verbal power of argument over "revolutionary tactics," also supported the war effort and nationalism though she was an avowed non-militant suffragist. However, there were other suffragists such as Sylvia Pankhurst (Emmeline Pankhurst's older daughter), Emily Hobhouse, Catherine Marshall, Helena Swanwick, Olive Schreiner, and Kate Courtney who were totally against the war. The pacifist suffragists saw militarism as yet another version of patriarchy, of the strong oppressing the weak; they believed women needed the vote to stop wars. Yet, although the suffragists were bitterly divided in their moral view of the war, they were united in the cause of women's emancipation. When, in the summer of 1916, it became clear that some kind of franchise bill was inevitable, suffrage societies all around the country mobilized the expressions of public support that were rising spontaneously on all sides so that Parliament should be well aware of this new climate of opinion. The societies sent deputations to their Members of Parliament, and the officers interviewed cabinet ministers (Strachey 1928, 354 et seq).

For the suffragists the war posed an immediate question, namely, what attitude should they take toward it? Emmeline Pankurst was recuperating at St. Malo when war was declared. In her biography of her mother, Sylvia Pankhurst writes that as Emmeline followed the people of St. Malo to hear the mayor read the declaration of war between France and Germany, she witnessed the grief of the old folk who remembered the war of 1870. "Her past reached out to her appealing memories; her own words rang in her ears: 'War is not women's way! To the women of this Union [Women's Social and Political Union WSPU] human life is sacred!'" (E. Sylvia Pankhurst 1936, 150). That week's issue of The Suffragette reiterated the idea that war was not women's way; its leading article was an appeal against the death-dealing militancy of men. The next week the paper did not appear. There had been urgent negotiations for the release of the suffragette prisoners, but the home secretary, Mr. McKenna, had refused to let them go, except under the pledge none of them would give: "not to commit further crimes or outrages." Suddenly McKenna released the prisoners, and on 13 August a proclamation suspended the activities of the WSPU with the words, " . . . we believe that under the joint rule of enfranchised women and men the nations of the world will, owing to women's influence and authority, find a way of reconciling the claims of peace and honour, and of regulating international relations without bloodshed . . . we ardently desire that our country shall be victorious—this because we hold that the existence of small nationalities is at stake . . . It will be the future task of women, and only they can perform it, to ensure that the present world tragedy . . . shall not be repeated" (Morgan 1975, 134–35). This is a far cry from Emmeline Pankhurst's actual behavior during the war.

In her biography of her mother, Sylvia writes that although "Mrs. Pankhurst devoted herself to the cause of winning the war with characteristic whole-heartedness, the propaganda of hate and bloodshed was alien to her inner spirit" (E. Sylvia Pankhurst 1937, 154). But according to others, the "Pankhurst organization" was always bellicose in tone (Morgan 1975, 136; Ramelson 1967,

154). Emmeline Pankhurst believed that to stand for Peace was the way to be abused and ostracized, and to take that way would rouse still fiercer opposition against the suffrage cause. Her daughter Sylvia was of quite the opposite opinion, much to her mother's dismay and eventual scorn. The announcement of 4 October 1915, heralding the amalgamation of *The Suffragette* into *Britannia*, makes clear her commitment to feminist rights and militarism: "In the name of British Women's equality of political right and duty, and also as a pledge of devotion to the nation of which we are privileged to be members" (Morgan 1975, 136–37).

For Emmeline Pankhurst then, as for her younger daughter, Christabel, but not for her older daughter Sylvia, militant patriotism and expedient politics united to build an overwhelming case for suffrage. Millicent Fawcett was another who never ceased to hold this view. Although she was an antimilitant suffragist, she was a prowar nationalist; however, not everyone in the National Union of Women's Suffrage Societies (NUWSS or National Union) agreed with her. Feminists in many countries were horrified by the disastrous war and tried to find ways to end it. Although president of the International Suffrage Peace Association, Fawcett refused to sign the proposal for a Women's Peace Conference to be held at The Hague in April–May 1915.

In February 1915, the National Union's council met for the first time under war conditions. Knowing that many of the women present disagreed with her, Fawcett stated quite categorically that until German troops were out of France and Belgium, it was treason to speak of peace. The result of this open challenge was that all the officers and ten of the executive committee resigned in protest.[5] Fawcett's attitude towards the prewar militants and wartime pacifists is contradictory; but she clearly believed patriotism and militarism took precedence over the emancipation issue for the duration of the war. In a message to the members of her National Union she declared:

> Women, your country needs you. As long as there was any hope for peace, most members of the National Union probably sought for peace, and endeavoured to support those who were trying to maintain it. But we have another duty now. . . . Let us show ourselves worthy of citizenship, whether our right to it be recognised or not. (Strachey 1931, 276)

Although Fawcett was left with only a few supporters at headquarters, her support in the country with rank and file members was strong. After Fawcett's brusque rejection of their differences, those who resigned from the National Union helped to assist in promoting The Hague Peace Conference of 1915. According to Sylvia Pankhurst, The Hague Conference:

> clove in twain the feminist movement of the world. . . We in the East End supported it; my name went forward as a delegate. Adela in Australia, and the Women's Party there . . . adhered to the Congress. Mrs. Pankhurst and Christabel brought the W.S.P.U. to life again to oppose it. Mrs. Pankhurst announced her return to the platform to stimulate war enthusiasm and to recruit men for the Army. (E. Sylvia Pankhurst 1936, 152–53).

If Emmeline Pankhurst thought militancy a virtue before the war, and the motto of the WSPU was "Deeds not Words," both she and Millicent Fawcett saw militarism as a virtue during the war. To some extent they were right, for it was the fear of women's return to militancy that influenced the prime minister, Asquith, and men like Lord Cromer and Lord Balfour of Burleigh to change their minds in favor of women's suffrage. The war was less important for altering the validity of antisuffrage arguments than for transforming the political climate in which they were voiced. As Lord Balfour later recalled, "I think really what happened was that the War gave a very good excuse to a large number of excellent people, who had up to that time been on the wrong side, to change their minds" (Harrison 1978, 204). In short, it took a long time for the government to be aware that women were courageous, and an even longer time to convince it that women should have the vote. The government also feared a massive women's peace vote. It did not seem to occur to anyone that if women were divided in their views on the war, they might be equally divided in their votes and not vote en bloc.

Jingoism and White Feathers

Moreover, there was the voice of belligerent nationalism expressed by the militant suffragists like Emmeline and Christabel Pankhurst. These women raised their voices against women like Emily Hobhouse, Olive Schreiner, Kate Courtney, Chrystal Macmillan, and Helena Swanwick who were dedicated to fighting not the war itself, but the war mentality and the excessive propaganda and patriotic fervor, of the militant suffragist—Emmeline

Pankhurst herself, for instance and Millicent Fawcett—and the jingoism of Mrs. Alexander Ward, Mrs. Herman, and Jessie Pope. It was militant suffragists who handed out white feathers to men not in uniform.[6] These women seemed unconcerned at the quite frequent mistakes they made, like giving feathers to soldiers on leave and to those invalided out for nonvisible injuries.

Before military conscription became law in May 1916, some women helped organize mass recruitment meetings, urging men to join up. Emmeline and Christabel Pankhurst were extremely active in this cause. Emmeline in particular devoted much of her time to the recruiting platforms, and in 1915 *The Suffragette* changed its name to *Britannia* and according to Maria Ramelson, "became one of the most ferocious advocates of military conscription for men, industrial conscription for women, the internment of all people of enemy race of whatever age, and the more ruthless enforcement of the blockade against enemy and neutral nations" (Ramelson 1967, 167). When Sylvia Pankhurst addressed an anticonscription meeting in Trafalgar Square in the spring of 1916, her mother publicly rebuked her. Emmeline Pankhurst was in America at the time, but the *Britannia* issue of 28 April 1916, published the following paragraph:

> Hearing of a demonstration recently in Trafalgar Square, Mrs. Pankhurst, who is at present in America, sent the following cable: "Strongly repudiate and condemn Sylvia's foolish and unpatriotic conduct. Regret I cannot prevent use of name. Make this public."

That women handed out white feathers to men not in uniform is undoubtedly true. These women, according to Mitchell and Raeburn, seemed to regard this activity as necessary war work. In handing out white feathers and so playing on men's fear of cowardice by embarrassing them, these women were actually encouraging that most pernicious tradition whereby men see war as a necessary event for proving their manhood.

The Antiwar Suffragists

However, not all activist suffragists threw their weight behind the war effort; to some of the more idealistic leaders like Emily Hobhouse, Helena Swanwick, and Sylvia Pankhurst, war work was nothing more than capitulating to the argument for physical force; the whole point of democracy was that government no longer rested on brute strength but on the consent of the governed, and it represented a higher stage of civilization. "The extent of the movement to keep Britain out of the war is often overlooked," Jo Vellacott Newberry wrote in a seminal 1977 article in *History*.[7] A peace rally arranged by the NUWSS involving women from Hungary, France, Holland, and England, who were in London for a meeting of the International Women's Suffrage Alliance was actually going on at Kingsway Hall on 4 August 1914, and resolutions were passed against the war.

By the time the meeting concluded, the Liberal government had declared war on Britain's behalf. Clearly citizenship for these women was the first condition for enabling them to attain a collective influence on their society and on their own destinies.

As the war went on women like Olive Schreiner, Helena Swanwick, Emily Hobhouse, Catherine Marshall, and Ellen Key combined their demand for suffrage with their demand for peace; their disaffection revealed significant changes in their previous attitudes toward war. As Helena Swanwick states the position in her essay "Women and War," people who desire enfranchisement of women will only be effective workers if they work for pacifism, or the control of physical by moral force. Pacifists will only be effective if they admit that women's claim for freedom is based on the same principle.[8] There is an important argument here, worth repeating, for militarism is a more emphatic form of patriarchy: the oppression of the weak by the strong. The feminist pacifists always saw this connection; for whether women were pacifists or militant suffragists, it was still the men in power who determined women's choices in this matter. War is a male invention; women would not need to be pacifists if male politicians were stopped from declaring war as the method of solving conflict.

But the majority of women in England and the other warring countries—France, Belgium, Germany, and Russia—were not prepared to take concerted action against the war. The hopes of peace which surely must have sprung each day from the hearts and minds of a great many women did not make themselves heard. Indeed, the majority of women made the view of men completely their own and seemed willing to continue the war to a "glorious end." As Ellen Key wrote in 1915:

> As long as women continue to believe "that war can never cease" they prove that they do not *will* it to cease. Nor did slavery and the pestilence cease until there were people who believed in their

abolition. . . . Therefore, the first condition of the woman's peace movement is, that all talk of the necessity of war, the ennobling influence, the beauty, and the eternity of war should be silenced on the lips of women; that their lips should never be opened except to proclaim that war belongs to those phases of life that must be conquered if humanity is to be humanized. (Key 1916, 238–39).

Later she states that even if woman gains the vote, its value for human evolution depends on woman's making herself "free from passionate nationalism to which she during the war has succumbed as much as man" (Key 1916, 246).

The First International Women's Peace Conference 1915

The Women's International Conference held at The Hague, 28 April to 1 May, 1915, was a gathering from twelve countries of over one hundred fifty organizations; 1,136 participated as voting members with more than three hundred visitors and observers. The conference fully justified the hopes and faith of the conveners, in spite of the vociferous opposition from the British militant suffragists: "We suffragettes are no believers in that sham" (Wiltsher 1985, 83).

In Germany, the most powerful and largest women's organization, the nationalist middle-class BDF (Bund Deutscher Frauenvereine) and their leader, Gertrud Bäumer, did not recognize the conference. There was in fact a striking parallel between Emmeline Pankhurst's WSPU and Millicent Fawcett's NUWSS and the BDF: all were mostly middle class, and all opposed pacifism, ostensibly fearing such activity would jeopardize women's eventual emancipation.

To certain sections of the world's press and public opinion, the aims of the congress seemed either laughable or deplorable. The women were called foolish and naive; interfering and ill-informed; irresponsibly feminine, and at the same time boldly unwomanly. The quality of the delegations soon gave the lie to these smear campaigns.

Amongst the influential German delegation was the first woman judge in Germany, Dr. Anita Augspurg; and with her a pioneer feminist and trade-union organizer from Bavaria, Lida Gustava Heymann. Augspurg and Heymann were two of the most radical German feminists and leaders of the 2,000-strong Women's Suffrage League, which provided strong links between

feminism and pacifism. These women were fully aware of the
menacing role that militarism played in the German climate of
opinion, which was heavily against female suffrage. In Germany
the general perception of these radical feminists was that they
were dangerously international in their thinking, and eventually
the authorities banned all their meetings from March 1916
onward.

There were many other important international women present at The Hague Conference. Rosika Schwimmer of Hungary
was a striking and powerful woman with a world reputation
in suffragist and pacifist movements. Chrystal Macmillan was a
brilliant lawyer. From America came not only Jane Addams, who
chaired the congress and who was a woman with an international reputation as social philosopher, but also Emily Greene
Balch, professor of economics at Wellesley College (Bussey and
Tims 1980, 20). Both Addams and Balch were subsequently
awarded the Nobel Peace Prize in 1931 and 1946 respectively.
On leaving New York for the congress, Jane Addams told the
press she thought it valuable for women to state a new point of
view and "take counsel to see what may be done," although "We
do not think we can settle the war. We do not think that by
raising our hands we can make the armies cease slaughter"
(Wiltsher 1985, 86).

In her opening address, Dr. Aletta Jacobs (Holland's first
woman doctor), made the purpose of the congress clear:

> Those of us who have convened this Congress . . . have never called
> it a *Peace Congress*, but an International Congress of Women, assem-
> bled to protest against war, and to suggest steps which may lead to
> warfare becoming an impossibility. (Bussey and Tims 1980, 19 and
> *Towards Permanent Peace* 1915, 12)

Dr. Jacobs was anxious that the women gathered there should
not be accused of betraying their countries in a time of war by
advocating "peace at any price." However, the congress had
grown out of the International Suffrage Alliance, an already well-
established organization before the war, with a strong pacifist
bias in its leadership.

The pacifist suffragists did not put all the blame for World War
I on the ill-will of the enemy or on the stupidity of their own
male politicians. No, they admitted that women's indifference in
working for the cause of peace was also largely to blame, as the

following excerpts from the records of the International Congress at The Hague, chaired by Jane Addams, May 1915, show:

> Women of the warring countries have not only pawned their gold and jewels for the war, but they have urged their sons and husbands to enlist, and they are willing to lose, to sacrifice all, rather than that their country should fail to crush the enemy. (Sewall 1915, 235)

And Emily Hobhouse asked a vital question about women's responsibility in the matter of war:

> Where are the women? Should they not be united in an inter-national host against the suicide of Europe, and demand a peace that does not entail the subjugation of any nation, and save for humanity the lives that the war will demand to the end? (Hobhouse, in Sewall 1915, 236)[9]

And Olive Schreiner, who in her eloquent *Woman and Labour* (1911) had convincingly shown that men and women are absolutely interdependent and that it is society—not individual men—that controls women's lives, making them dependent as wives, mothers, and workers, addressed the congress in strong language:

> We, the bearers of men's bodies, who supply its most valuable munition, who . . . shed our blood and face death that the battlefield may have its food, a food more precious to us than our heart's blood; it is we especially who, in the domain of war, have our word to say, a word no man can say for us. . . . War will pass when intellectual culture and activity have made possible to the female an equal share in the control and governance of modern national life. (ibid., 235)

Alice Park sums up the argument, one which it would seem no woman could refute:

> The present situation offers many lessons to suffragists. There are many pitfalls at our feet. The women in Europe, whose motherlands are engaged in strife, are all alike in their voteless conditions. Like us, their hands are clean; they have no responsibility for this war. Like us, they have to pay the price nonetheless to the last farthing. They have to deliver up the sons they bore in agony to a bloody death in a quarrel of which they know not the why nor the wherefore, on the side of the particular ally their government has chosen for the moment; they face starvation at home for themselves and their children; meanwhile, many of them are exposed with their helpless

daughters to the lust and outrages of war-maddened soldiery. This
is what in cold fact war means to women. It is an aspect that the
world's press disregards, because it would make war unpopular. . . .
Until peace is established, it is our duty to press on with unabated
energy, to increase our activities at this crisis, to preach peace, sanity
and suffrage.[10]

Nevertheless, the prowar suffragists did not accept this argument for peace because unlike their pacifist sisters, they saw
their war work as one means of obtaining the vote, whereas the
pacifists saw the vote as a way of preventing war as a trial for
anything: humanity, glory, or emancipation. Although the congress did not produce any change of policy by the Allies or the
Germans, the women members returned to their countries with
a new enthusiasm, which spread to other women. According to
a report on the congress: "Hundreds of women in Great Britain
were convinced that their work lay not only in the relief of physical distress and suffering, but that upon them, as women and
non-combatants, fell especially the duty of preparing the way
for a better understanding and lasting peace between nations."
(Swanwick 1915, 15).

As Frau Keilhau, the Norwegian delegate, emphasized, the congress was of historical importance because up till then women
had not taken any responsibility in questions of war. "But now
women of the world had for the first time met to protest against
this horrible evil" (ibid., 8). Roughly speaking, there were two
elements in the congress, those who took the Quaker point of
view and were anxious for an unqualified "Stop the War" resolution; and those who felt that the congress was definitely not a
"Stop the War" congress and that a resolution demanding peace
could not be passed without some statement as to terms by the
1,136 voting members. Eventually, a resolution entitled "The
Peace Settlement" was finally agreed upon. It urged all governments of the world to begin peace negotiations based upon the
principles of justice, including the denial of the right of con-
quest. This latter point was particularly important to the Belgian
and French women at the congress. The resolution also included
a demand that women be given equal political rights with men
and demands for universal disarmament, democratic control of
foreign policy, and the establishment of a permanent international conference with women and men equally represented.

After the conference, speaking to a large gathering of women
at the Kingsway Hall in London on 13 May, Kate Courtney, one

of the few English delegates who managed to attend the congress (in spite of the channel ports being closed by the government to prevent the women attending, and, furthermore, the official refusal to issue more than twenty-four passports to the 180 women wanting to attend the congress), emphasized "that suffering united all the nationalities, belligerent and neutral—but especially did it unite the delegates of the countries warring against one another."

Courtney went on to mention another tie, and a new one—the feeling of "women's responsibility" (Swanwick 1915, 21). The more strongly women felt responsibility for the war, the more urgent became their demand for political emancipation. Here it must be admitted that, although women were voteless before the war, they shared collective responsibility to some extent for the climate of opinion which had made the war possible. In the future, peace would be the work of men and women acting in cooperation. Thus these pacifist suffragists meeting at The Hague in April 1915 not only voiced their disaffection with the war because of their traditional role as nurturers and carers of the human race, but also because of their changed and changing perception of themselves as a decisive political and moral force.

The congress did not get a good press in Britain; indeed the press set out to prove that the congress had been as futile a proceeding as they had predicted it would be. As Evelyn Sharp, writing on "The Congress and the Press," comments, the press cuttings will sound as familiar to every woman reformer as to her:

> "Blundering Englishwomen" *(Daily Graphic)*
> "This mischievous and futile committee" *(Globe)*
> "Folly in Petticoats" *(Sunday Pictorial)*
> "The babblers from his country" *(Evening Standard)*
> "This shipload of hysterical women" (William le Queux in *The Globe)*
> "Pro-Hun Peacettes in their 6th floor eyrie" *(Daily Express)*
> "This Spring Jaunt to anxious neutral Holland" *Eastbourne Chronicle)*

And she goes on to say, "As in all progressive movements, however, it is fear that really runs through this outcry of the Press— fear lest the women might perhaps be right, might perhaps impress their belief on the women of other belligerent countries, might perhaps make this war really 'the last war' instead of merely talking about it as an unattainable ideal very useful as a

recruiting cry" (Sharp 1915, 22–23). The most invidious statement she quotes is from the *Sunday Times* and serves as a clear
though unintentional warning that women must be emancipated
and politically free to act and speak their minds:

> Doubtless amateurish peace projects need not be taken too seriously,
> but the impression on some of the observers of the proceedings was
> that the Governments of the world—both neutral and belligerent—
> would do well to put a quiet check on such schemes, lest they add
> to the embarrassments of the situation already difficult and delicate.
> (ibid., 23)

One of the most important outcomes of this first international
women's peace congress was the formation in 1919 of The
Women's International League for Peace and Freedom (WILPF),
an organization that has—ever since and continuing into the
present—sought to establish the conditions for a just and durable
peace. Little did those courageous farseeing women who met at
The Hague during the First World War think that their spirit of
international cooperative humanism and feminism would result
in a worldwide organization with branches in many countries
on many continents.

Public Perceptions of Pacifism, 1914–1918

During the First World War, many considered pacifist suffragists as unpatriotic, even traitorous, and this became a more hardened view after a German submarine torpedoed the Cunard
passenger ship *Lusitania*, the largest passenger ship afloat. Ironically, the catastrophe happened just after the Women's Hague
Peace Conference. The ship was voyaging from New York to Liverpool when it was sunk off the western coast of Ireland on
Friday, 7 May 1915, resulting in the loss of over a thousand of
the two thousand people on board, many of them women and
children.[11] This unprecedented disaster caused deep revulsion
on both sides of the Atlantic, and in England it resulted in an
enormous feeling of public outrage and hostility against anything
German. German stores were damaged and looted in the East End
of London, and there was a public demand for the internment of
all Germans as enemy aliens. Nineteen thousand enemy aliens
had already been interned, but Prime Minister Asquith had to
concede to public opinion in the matter. He announced the

repatriation of old men, women, and children, and the further internment of young men of military age. And this was before the first battle of the Somme in July 1916, when the public was further stunned and outraged by the enormous casualty figures Germany inflicted upon the British Army: twenty thousand dead in a single day and forty thousand casualties (Charman 1975, 75).

It is probable that any all-out effort by pacifist suffragist women to communicate with "enemy women" after 1915–16 would have resulted in a backlash against emancipation by the general public.[12] In chapters two and three of *Troublesome People: The Warriors of Pacifism*, Caroline Moorehead gives a detailed account of the hostility and ridicule male pacifists were subject to during the war by the Tribunals set up to hear their case, by the general British public who referred to them as "conchies" and the "won't-fight funks," as well as by the army whose treatment of them was both brutal and shameful (29–56).[13] But these convinced pacifists were motivated by a passionate belief in political negotiation as a nonviolent means of effecting political change and/or compromise; such a stance requires courage, especially in wartime when the spirit of revenge hovers heavily in the air.

As David Mitchell points out, for many women the war was something of a paradox (1965, 34). It was the product of blundering male politicians, of male thinking; it was therefore a disgrace and might never have happened if women had been given their fair share in policy making. Christabel Pankhurst wrote in an article to *The Suffragette*, August 1914: "As I write a dreadful war-cloud seems about to burst and deluge the peoples of Europe with fire, slaughter, ruin . . . this then is the world as men have made it, life as men have ordered it" (Ramelson 1967, 166).

But not all men, of course. Writing in the early 1990s, it seems to me it is no longer possible to share entirely this view of Christabel's. Anyone familiar with the history of pacifism during the last seventy years will find that men have also consistently written pacifist texts and taken pacifist action. Many of the men who fought in World War I became ardent antiwar activists in the late twenties and thirties. The Non-Conscription League was organized by men as was the Fellowship for Reconciliation. There were roughly two thousand conscientious objectors in World War I; approximately six thousand in World War II. Two million men signed the first disarmament petition submitted to the League of Nations in 1931. And after the Second World War and the invention of nuclear weapons, men and women combined their voices and efforts against the ultimate force that can still destroy us all.

It is no longer possible to assume that the majority of women have been more consistently antimilitaristic than men. It is true that men are the historic authors of the violence of war, but women have participated and been drawn in, in many ways. Still it is men who have mostly described and defined war; women, on the whole, who have reacted. But there is the question of historic female violence and how we have read it. There is no evidence that allows us to suppose that there is less revenge-fulness in women than in men. In her social and cultural history of women and war, Elshtain suggests that female violence is always seen as an aberration, whereas male violence "could be *moralized* as a structured activity—war—and thus be depersonalized and idealized" (1987, 169).[14] We will return to this subject later.

It was the writers among the pacifist suffragists who voiced the keenest outrage at the war in an effort to build solidarity with those women who shared the same feelings but would not voice them. How could they?—most of them were engaged in war work of one kind or another. Thousands of these women, perhaps millions if one includes the women of Belgium, France, Germany, and Russia, must have been heartsore; but for the most part they were silent, especially at the beginning of the war. They had a deep sense of loyalty to their men and were acutely aware of their sufferings and sacrifices. Not for the world would they say anything that would seem to undervalue their men, or suggest that they were being sacrificed for a wrong or mistaken cause. So in backing the men who were actually fighting in the war, many women seemed to be backing warfare itself, although most probably they abhorred it. They were caught in the classic situation of women whose men are away at war.

Winning the Vote: June 1917

While the suffrage cause took second place to winning the war and/or producing the peace, the suffrage societies, "upwards of forty," still maintained their organizations. The pacifist suffragists, led by women like Sylvia Pankhurst in her East End Settlement and Emily Hobhouse and The Women's International League, directed their energies towards peaceful settlement and war relief, whilst their sisters such as Emmeline and Christabel

Pankhurst put their energies into the war effort. Both groups kept their eyes on what could be done to ensure adequate training for women to keep the suffrage issue alive and visible. In the summer of 1916, busy as they were with their war work, suffrage societies from all over the country found time to send deputations to Westminster to ensure that if there were a new franchise bill when Asquith's government fell, women's suffrage should be part of it.

On 14 August Asquith himself gave up his opposition to women's suffrage. "It is true," he said, "that women cannot fight in the sense of going out with rifles and so forth, but . . . they have aided in the most effective way in the prosecution of the war. What is more—and this is a point which makes a special appeal to me—they say when the war comes to an end . . . when the process of industrial reconstruction has to be set on foot, have not the women a special claim to be heard on the many questions which will arise directly affecting their interest? . . . I say quite frankly that I cannot deny that claim" (E. Sylvia Pankhurst 1931, 600; Strachey 354). Evidently it was the militants who persuaded Asquith, not the pacifists. Ironically, when Christabel Pankhurst stood for the Women's Party in December 1918 in the first general election in which women could vote and stand as candidates, she was perceived as being too militant.

On June 19, 1917, the Representation of the People bill, with its controversial Clause IV (Woman's Suffrage) was passed with an overwhelming majority of 385 to 55 against (Strachey 1928, 361). The bill passed its third reading on 7 December 1917, giving the vote to women over thirty and to all men over twenty-one. (It was not until 1928 that women were given the vote at twenty-one.) As Sylvia Pankhurst, among others, writes, "Undoubtedly the large part taken by women during the War in all branches of social service had proved a tremendous argument for their enfranchisement" (E. Sylvia Pankhurst 1931, 607).

After the war was over, no doubt most women hoped that the future would corroborate the opinion of Helena Swanwick:

> The war has been the most terrible shock to all thinking women. Instinct alone will no longer suffice. They must attain a new certainty through an attitude that *puts them in relation to society.* [my emphasis] Some of us feel that we are mere checkers [sic] for the politicians and we are beside ourselves at the thought that they claim the privilege of destroying our life, our work, our hopes, our children, the very people whose protectors we are. (Swanwick 1972, 30)

Against the massive destructiveness of war women had to and did take a stand.[15] During World War I women stood up and made themselves heard, realizing they could no longer afford to be mere onlookers in a man's world. The suffragist movement, both militant and pacifist, recognized the immense potential in feminist intervention to alter the prevailing image of women— as women and political voices. Pacifist women like Helena Swanwick believed that once the vote put women in a rational relation to society, women's political and moral commitment must be to help establish a new system of values based on cooperation, not domination and subordination.

In Great Britain it took just over fifty years to win the first victory, and a further ten before men and women were equal as voting citizens, that is from the presentation of the first petition to Parliament by John Stuart Mill and Henry Fawcett on 7 June 1866, to the royal assent given on February 6, 1918, to the government's Representation of the People act. Although there is a wide variety of opinion as to how much World War I contributed to women's emancipation, it is undeniably true that the years between 1914 and 1918 transformed the whole situation, making it impossible to continue in the old way with a restricted men's franchise. As Constance Rover writes:

> It is frequently said that women were given the vote "because of the war" and while this is indeed true, one may safely conclude that the vote would not have been gained at that time, had it not been demanded, very emphatically, in the pre-war years. (Rover 1967, 205)

In his chapter, "War and Suffrage," Morgan agrees in this summing up:

> If the impact of war on party politics and necessities was the principal cause of Suffrage success in 1918, it is as well to note that Woman Suffragists had brought their issue to the point where it became one of those necessities. (1975, 149–50)[16]

As indicated earlier, both the militant and pacifist suffragists recognized that feminist intervention could alter prevailing images of women. During the period from 1900 to 1914 the militant suffragists recognized patriarchy as the enemy to be defeated, and they courageously fought this enemy; however, when the war came, they supported the patriarchal system with their own militarism. It was the pacifist suffragists who recognized militarism as another emphatic form of patriarchy, and they, in their turn, bravely stood up against this same system. They were also motivated by humane principles: reverence for all life and abhorrence of the violent destructiveness of war. The experience of change caused by the suffrage movement together with the effect of the war upon women's lives transformed women's image of themselves in radical and irreversible ways.

War poetry seems to be the literary form that offers the most condensed and deepest insight into the human response to war. The next chapter focuses on some of the women and men poets of World War I, both famous and obscure, and the lasting impression offered by their poetry of what it was like to live through those changing and tragic times as women and men. Both views are necessary for a full understanding of the significance of war in the lives of human beings.

2

British Women Poets and Soldier Poets of World War I

"I am the enemy you killed, my friend"

To focus on the literature of women's experience of this disastrous war, I begin with an anthology of 125 poems by seventy-two women edited by Catherine Reilly—*Scars Upon My Heart: Women's Poetry and Verse of the First World War* (1981; hereafter referred to as *Scars*). Although the war ended sixty-three years before its publication, the anthology is the first of its kind.[1] As Reilly points out in her introduction, the anthologies of Great War poetry published in recent years tend to concentrate on the soldier poets who served on the western front, poets like Sassoon, Owen, Bridges, Rosenberg, Read, and Blunden.[2] It is indeed hard to recall that there were women poets of the First World War, even when reading such a comprehensive book as Paul Fussell's *The Great War and Modern Memory* (1975) or John Johnston's *English Poetry of the First World War* (1964) or Bernard Bergonzi's *Heroes' Twilight* (1965). However, recent scholarship by women is beginning to redress this imbalance.[3]

Judith Kazantzis's preface to *Scars* suggests that the near total disappearance of women's World War I poetry has perhaps had to do with a lasting feeling that women never had any real right to speak out against a cataclysm that left most of them safely at home. However, a great many women on the home front who were writers and suffragists did speak out, as the previous chapter has shown, and thousands of others went to France as nurses and ambulance drivers. Perhaps the answer lies more in the fact that it is men who have made the anthologies, and in so doing they have consciously and/or unconsciously selected the masculine experience of the war, and by and large that has defined our

experience. Or perhaps since World War I was essentially a man's
world and women never experienced the actual battlefield and
its scenes of horror and devastation—never experienced the kind
of anger, fear, and frustration that the men felt in the trenches,
conveyed to us by poets like Sassoon and Owen in particular—
they could not write about it.

On the other hand, in her discussion of the impact of the Great
War on women's sensibility and art Gilbert writes that although
women mourned the devastation of war, their literary art was
"subtly strengthened, or at least strangely inspired, by the deaths
and defeats of male contemporaries."[4] But this generalized claim
seems dubious.[5] Apart from the sense of personal loss and
grief—surely the decisive emotions—most women whether artists or not would not have felt this way. It is however quite probable, as Gilbert implies, that established female writers were
liberated by the war from the dominance of the male literary and
publishing world.

Vera Brittain in *Lady into Woman* (1953) speaks of the war
cutting men off from women because of their horrific knowledge,
and she believes that this knowledge created a permanent im-
pediment to understanding. This implies that men internalized
their war experience in various and different ways from women,
either by repressing it, which often resulted in psychic illness,
or, if they were writers or artists, by displacing it onto their
creative work. Freud was one of the first to appreciate the necessity of working through the repression of war trauma in order to
recover some sort of psychic wholeness.[6]

During the war, the problem of the gulf between what the men
were experiencing at the front and what the women were experiencing at home was compounded by men's transference of immense amounts of emotional energy from that home to the front.
The front became their home; their comrades, their family. Moreover, this "family" was being continually shattered, resulting in
perpetual grief and bereavement.[7] In *Good-bye To All That*, Robert Graves says grimly that "The average life expectancy of an
infantry subaltern on the Western Front was, at some stages of the
War, only about three months" (59). The day-by-day mourning of
dead comrades and the imminence of one's own death were psychic catastrophes women were mercifully spared.

Women did not then, as some feminists such as Kahn, Higonnet, Gilbert, and Gubar desired and still desire, write out of direct
personal experience of the trenches. When they did write of
trench warfare it was mostly from their imaginative understand-

ing of its horrors, not of its comradeship. They had other agonies to write about. Ample evidence of these other feminine experiences of the war appears in Reilly's anthology, Scars, which gives a representative voice to what women felt and thought during this great catastrophe, both behind the lines in France and on the home front.

Margaret Higonnet writes that the "anxiety of authorship" caused some of the women writers in Scars to "ventriloquize" (1987, 14) in order to represent the blood and mud which they themselves did not experience. I would say rather that these women poets used their active imaginations. To imagine the battlefield and all that went on there, intellectually, emotionally, and militarily, is not to ventriloquize but to get nearer the poetic truth. Higonnet supports her view by citing Cicely Hamilton's poem, "Non-Combatant" (Scars, 46), but her interpretation seems too selective. The poet requires the reader to understand not only the "useless mouth" (the "ventriloquist's") of stanza two, but also the "aimless hands" of stanza four and the "stiffened lip" of stanza five as acknowledgments, even apologies, for her absence from the battle front (and thus her failure to risk life and limb), for whatever reason, including prevention by patriarchal authority.

Gilbert and Gubar have also written about various kinds of anxiety women authors experienced at this time. They seem to share the opinion that "Since the definition of war poetry privileges actual battlefront experience, women who are barred from combat can only participate in this literary mode at secondhand" (Higonnet 1987, 14). I would argue that that is only one definition of war poetry, and that the poems in the anthology Scars offer several more equally valid definitions of war poetry by women of all ages and from many different social backgrounds. For example, there is the poetry of grief, mourning, and loss, mostly in elegiac form; the poetry of protest, containing strong ideological statements; and the poetry of survival, often in sonnet form.

As we shall see later in the chapter, it was the nurses of Voluntary Aid Detachments (hereafter referred to as VADs) who came closest to experiencing the actual trauma of the battlefront while caring for the shocking mutilations the soldiers had to endure. Some of these nurses expressed their experience in poetry. The poems of May Sinclair, Eva Dobell, and Mary Henderson—all to be found in Scars—express deep anxiety and overwhelming horror at the monstrous wounds the battlefield inflicted upon the men's bodies and minds.

Here it is worth noting that from 31 March 1917, there were women other than nurses engaged in noncombatant duties on lines of communication in France. After the terrible casualties endured by the British army in 1915 and 1916, it was decided that 12,000 soldiers engaged in noncombatant duties in France could be replaced by women. This situation led to the formation of the Women's Army Auxiliary Corps. The corps, whose chief controller was Mrs. Chalmers Watson, C.B.E., was a great success and was renamed Queen Mary's Army Auxiliary Corps. In *Women In Uniform* Collett Wadge writes of the WAACs, "Before demobilization 57,000 British women went through the ranks, 10,000 of them serving in the western theatre of war" (12).

In her recent book on women poets of Word War I, Kahn (1988) includes women poets not collected in *Scars*, but regrettably many of these other poems are not easy for the general reader to locate. *Scars* is still the most useful single comprehensive source and poetic narrative for understanding the response of women in Britain to the impact of World War I. Although the poems vary in skill and form, they convey a moving and sometimes eloquent account of women's lives as mothers, wives, sisters, lovers, munition workers, nurses, ambulance drivers, and pacifist and militant suffragists. The war influenced every aspect of women's lives; and the themes of guilt, despair, protest, grief, lament, and reconciliation to a bitter and sometimes even shameful survival constitute the narrative of the anthology as a whole.

Scars Upon My Heart: August 1914 to Spring 1915

Let us now consider some of the women's poems in *Scars*, and by way of comparison poems of some of their male contemporaries, the "soldier poets." At the beginning of the war, early in 1915, Rose Macaulay wrote painfully and exactly about the imagined barriers that cut women off from the front line experience of war. In "Picnic" she expresses the frustration, anguish, and guilt at staying home:

> And life was bound in a still ring,
>   Drowsy, and quiet, and sweet . . .
> When heavily up the south-east wind
>   The great guns beat.

The women are still part of the ethos that seeks to protect them from the obscenity of war, although this exclusion from witnessing the actual battle scenes cannot shield them, especially the poets among them, from the anxiety of imaging and dreaming of these scenes:

> We are shut about by guarding walls:
>   (We have built them lest we run
> Mad from dreaming of naked fear
>   And of black things done).
>
> (Scars, 67)

Emily Hobhouse, although a minority voice, had already written strong words about the "protection" of women in wartime: "Are not men victims of a fallacy when they seek to justify their combative instincts by declaring they must 'protect' their women and children? Is it not time to expose this fallacy? For do they succeed in their aim? Even if they did succeed do we women wish to be thus protected at the cost of other people's lives and widespread misery and destruction? Many brave women openly object, and with one voice shall we not all assert that we do not want that kind of protection; it savours of barbarism?" Here, it is the male concept of womanly protection itself that is being challenged, on moral and psychological grounds. The point of view represents a significant shift in the female perception of masculine authority and in the effect of that authority upon women's moral and political activities. The argument is that morally war is the responsibility of women as well as men.

Some of the most powerful images of trench warfare were the mud, the rats and blood. In "Picnic" Macaulay goes on to use another image of war which women writers of World War I mention more often than the men: pain. In some respects it was no doubt easier for the men bravely to suffer pain than for their womenfolk to endure helplessly the thought of their suffering. The images of pastoral England, of gentleness, fertility, and growth, change into images of rage and pain as Macaulay thinks of the anguish of the men lying in their own blood in the mud of Flanders:

> And far and far are Flanders mud,
>   And the pain of Picardy;
> And the blood that runs there runs beyond
>   The wide waste sea.
>
> (Scars, 67)

Here the poet envisions a sea of blood far exceeding Macbeth's guilt. When the soldier poets use the image of blood it is not so much to suggest flow as color, or the lack of it, in soldiers bleeding to death. Poets like Sassoon and Owen make the reader sense blood's physical qualities: its color, smell, and stickiness, as in the third stanza from Owen's "Insensibility":

> Happy are these who lose imagination:
> They have enough to carry with ammunition.
> Their spirit drags no pack,
> Their old wounds save with cold can not more ache.
> Having seen all things red,
> Their eyes are rid
> Of the hurt of the colour of blood for ever.
>
> (Owen 1931, 63)

One can account for the difference in the use of the image of blood in Macaulay's and Owen's poems simply by admitting that Macaulay had to imagine a truth about wounds to create her metaphor; whereas to Owen and other soldier poets the sight of blood was a daily, hourly reality, soaking into their imaginations.

Another recurring feminine image of the trenches is rain; when it rains in England it suggests more blood-soaked mud in the fields of Flanders. "Picnic" concludes:

> Be still, be still, south wind, lest your
>   Blowing should bring the rain. . . .
> We'll lie very quiet on Hurt Hill,
>   And sleep once again.
>
>
> Oh, we'll lie quite still, nor listen nor look,
>   While the earth's bounds reel and shake,
> Lest, battered too long, our walls and we
>   Should break . . . should break. . . .
>
> (Scars, 67)

Here the poet's words, "be still," "lie very quiet," "sleep," suggest a desire almost for suspended life—a need not to disturb the universe any more than necessary, or any more than it is already shocked and "hurt." There is a need not to "listen" or "look" at the catastrophe going on so geographically close to the women of England that they can feel the earth shaking under them from the same explosions that rock the men in their trenches. The word "battered" in the penultimate line suggests yet another identification with the soldiers at the front: not only the implacable destructiveness of the guns, which could be heard especially clearly in southern England when a south wind was blowing, but also the battering that women's hearts and minds were experiencing. Finally, the poem ends with the perception that the walls, real and imaginary, that have heretofore protected women from the hideous knowledge of war, can no longer hold up. There is the suggestion, perhaps, that women no longer want to wait cringing behind safe walls whilst their menfolk die in ditches.

Rain is an important ironic image in "July 1914," a poem by Anna Akhmatova, one of the only two women poets included in Jon Silkin's anthology, *First World War Poetry* (1979):

> From the burning woods drifts
> the sweet smell of juniper.
> Widows grieve over their brood,
> the village rings with their lamentation.
>
>
> If the land thirsted, it was not in vain,
> nor were the prayers wasted;
> for a warm red rain soaks
> the trampled fields.

> (Silkin 1979, 260)

In this context one thinks of Edith Sitwell's powerful poem of World War II, "Still Falls the Rain," in Catherine Reilly's anthology of women's poetry of World War II, *Chaos in the Night*. I shall explore this anthology in chapter 5.

Water is a powerful image for the women writers in *Scars*— especially the fusion of rain with blood and mud. Some religious writers see rain as "heavenly" and "healing" as in Charlotte Mew's "May 1915" (72) where blood washed away by rain is a libation. Rain is also associated with tears that wash, cleanse, and purify.

The image of rain is differently used by the soldier poets. In "Aftermath," Sassoon speaks of a "hopeless rain" coming in with "dirty-white" dawn, and Blunden writes of "the grey rain" in his poem "Third Ypres." Owen wrote to his mother from the Somme at the beginning of 1917: "The waders are of course indispensable. In two and a half miles of trench which I waded yesterday there was not one inch of dry ground. There is a mean depth of two feet of water" (Owen 1967, 426). Rain for these poets meant sodden boots and trench foot, drizzling daybreak over no-man's-land with its waterlogged shell craters and ever present sight of mutilated and decaying bodies of men sunk in the "sucking mud" and "slime." In Sassoon's first poem in *Counter-Attack*, published in 1918, he reveals a world whose inhabitants have been overwhelmed with unspeakable disaster:

> The place was rotten with dead; green clumsy legs
> High-booted, sprawled and grovelled along the saps
> And trunks, face downward, in the sucking mud,
> Wallowed like trodden sand-bags loosely filled;
> And naked sodden buttocks, mats of hair,
> Bulged, clotted heads slept in the plastering slime.
> And then the rain began,—the jolly old rain!

(36)

No woman could have written this so concretely. No woman had this combat experience (though whether or not some of them might have wanted it is not easy to be sure about). To the horrors of simple carnage are added the frantic, intermingled, struggling grotesqueries of violent death: the final degradation of the human body. Both men and women poets responded to the truth of the war as they perceived it: truth compounded of brutality and horror, ignominy and death for the men, and for the women, outrage, fear, and grief. Not only did the men and women poets use the imagery of war differently; they used the language differently, too. Fussell (1975) gives a list of military feudal rhetoric in his chapter on "A Satire of Circumstance."[8] From this list it is clear that the soldier poets were writing within a tradition of war poetry with its own language. However, as the war and its appalling atrocities went on and on, poets like Owen, Blunden, Rosenberg, and Sassoon avoided the traditional vocabulary of "glorious," "heroic" war, using instead irony and restraint. Their language became as grim as no-man's-land, free from the bombastic rhetoric of the propagandist and the enervating romanticism of the sentimentalist.[9]

No such tradition of female war poetry was available to the British women poets of *Scars*, and the fact that they did not seek to adopt either the masculine traditional vocabulary or the realism of the soldier poets suggests a conscious forging of their own particular voices. The soldier poets saw the violence done to nature and to man as it was happening through the vile machinery of war; the women saw this violence as it affected them as nurses, mothers, wives, sisters, lovers, and activists. Both accounts are necessary for a full understanding of the significance of war for men and women.

In Kahn's (1988) attempt to claim poetic equality for the women poets with the soldier poets she ignores important and inevitable differences. Differences there were—in experience, perception, imagery, and language. The equality or similarity is in the subject matter, the war itself, but the gender responses are different for reasons I have already suggested, such as the historical, the political, and psychological factors as well as the division between the front-line and the home-front experience of the war. Above all, the responses of women and men poets together constitute the total account of this most horrendous disaster in which nearly ten million Allied, British, French, and German lives were sacrificed.

Another poem by Macaulay, "The Shadow," is remarkable for its almost apocalyptic vision of a zeppelin air raid and for its attempt to unite the civilian terror of air raids with the soldier's experience at the front. In a series of refrains which identify the civilian and military victims as one, the poem draws a parallel between the senseless death-dealing machine raining down destruction on the citizens of London with the deaths on the battlefields of France:

> There was a Shadow on the moon; I saw it poise
> and tilt, and go
> Its lonely way, and so I know that the blue velvet
> night will soon
> Blaze loud and bright, as if the stars were crashing
> right into the town,
> And tumbling streets and houses down,
> and smashing people like wine jars . . .

> *Fear wakes:*
> *What then?*
> *Strayed shadow of the Fear that breaks*
> *The world's young men.*

> (Scars, 67–68)

Again, as with "Picnic" there is a sense of a violent cosmic disturbance: the universe falling in on itself, collapsing all life and emptying it of meaning. Although this upheaval brings fear, it is not a fear that mobilizes, but one that paralyzes.

Last time they came they messed our square, and left it a hot
    rubbish-heap,
With people sunk in it so deep, you could not even hear them
    swear.

> Fire blinds.
> What then?
> Pale shadow of the Pain that grinds
>   The world's young men.

(Scars, 68)

Here is a suggestion of the bestiality of war; "messed our square"
has thoroughly unpleasant implications which connect it with
the suggestion that the mess is a garbage heap made of human
beings.

The weak blood running down the street, oh, does it run like
    fire, like wine?
Are the split brains so keen, so fine, crushed limbs so swift,
    dead dreams so sweet?
There is a Plain where limbs and dreams and brains to set the
    world a-fire
Lie tossed in sodden heaps of mire. . . . Crash! Tonight's show
    begins, it seems.

> Death. . . . Well,
> What then?
> Rim of the shadow of the Hell
>   Of the world's young men.

(Scars, 68)

In the penultimate verse an identification is made between
civilian victims of war on the home front and the soldiers on
the battlefield. Large numbers of both groups end up in a pile of
indiscriminate mutilations. The imagery details the pain of war
and its devastating effect on the human body, its horrifying capacity to crush limbs, spill brains, and smash buildings and even
civilization itself; moreover, this hell is man-made. The debate
about women's place being in the home is at its most paradoxical
during wartime, especially during air raids on cities and towns
where in fact the home might be the most dangerous of places.[10]
    Like Rose Macaulay, Alice Meynell in her poem "Summer in
England 1914" tries to reconcile the irreconcilable experiences

of women at the beginning of the war: their existence in the
loveliness of pastoral England with their knowledge of the obscenity of life in the trenches.

> Most happy year! And out of town
>   The hay was prosperous, and the wheat;
> The silken harvest climbed the down:
>   Moon after moon was heavenly-sweet,
> Stroking the bread within the sheaves
> Looking 'twixt apples and their leaves.

> And while this rose made round her cup,
>   The armies died convulsed. And when
> This chaste young silver sun went up
>   Softly, a thousand shattered men,
> One wet corruption, heaped the plain.
> After a league-long throb of pain.

> Flower following tender flower; and birds,
>   And berries; and benignant skies
> Made thrive the serried flocks and herds.—
>   Yonder are men shot through the eyes.
>   Love, hide thy face
> From man's unpardonable race.

                                              (Scars, 73)

Time and again in this anthology England is seen ironically
as a magnificent garden where everything grows abundantly (August 1914 was an exceptionally hot, sunny month)—everything
but love. The themes of nature and nurture are constantly contrasted with the martial values. In Meynell's poem the images of
food—bread, apples and berries, evidence of nature's fecun-
dity—are bitterly contrasted with the sterility and moral deprav-
ity of man when he is not one with nature, including human
nature. One is whole, the poet suggests, only when the soul is
in harmony with the landscape. This is also Blunden's theme in
many of his war poems; he is possibly the best nature poet of
the soldier poets. In his poem "Third Ypres" he best conveys the
sinister particulars of a war-ravaged landscape, ending with the
impressive antithetical line: "A whole sweet countryside amok
with murder" (Blunden, 1931, 156).
    The first stanza of Meynell's poem sets a scene of happiness

in the fruitfulness and interconnectedness of nature, culminating in the "silken harvest," a feminine image suggesting both gentleness and the preciousness of sustenance. The moonlight bathes the harvest almost as if blessing it. The use of moonlight here is in stark contrast to its use in Macaulay's "The Shadow" in which that light brings a harvest of death and destruction from the sky. (The people in the cities dreaded full moonlit nights, for then the zeppelins came.) In the second stanza the poet contrasts the natural cycle of the rose, a traditional symbol of love, with the unnatural ritual of war; as the life of a rose gradually unfolds, so the life of men in war is suddenly "convulsed" and "shattered." The "shattered men" on the plain of corruption suggest a grotesque, hideous compost heap of agonized humanity. The powerful last lines of the poem suggest both the blindness of the war mentality and one of its many obscenities: shooting a man's eyes out.

Poems after 1915

At the beginning of the war most women strained to identify with the male participants in any way they could, practically and imaginatively, but once the first appalling casualty lists came back after the battles of Ypres, Neuve-Chapelle, Aisne, and Loos in 1915, women's experience became one of increasing horror, loss, and grief, and it led to a desperate need to protest the war. Many of the poems written after 1915 are protest poems expressing outrage and anguish at the atrocious waste of life and the appalling suffering of the wounded in France. These poems voice the concerns of the antiwar suffragists, who became more and more vociferous as the war went on. According to Johnston (1964), it was Leslie Coulson who "strikes first and most clearly the keynote of protest and rejection that was to sound throughout the rest of the war" (75). Written only a few days before his death on 7 October 1916 at the age of nineteen, Coulson's "Who Made the Law?" wrathfully indicts both the senseless nature of the conflict and the unknown power whose ordinance permits it to continue:

> Who made the Law that men should die in meadows?
> Who spake the word that blood should splash in lanes?

Who gave it forth that gardens should be boneyards?
Who spread the hills with flesh, and blood, and brains?
Who made the Law?
(Johnston 1964, 74)

In a fascinating chapter in *The Great War and Modern Memory* (75–113), Fussell points out how the trench predicament dichotomized everything into them/us with no apparent hope of synthesis between those who did and did not experience life in the trenches. However, some men and women poets did write of a possible synthesis, although a tragic one, as in Owen's haunting "Strange Meeting," the last poem in Blunden's edition of his work (1931):

I am the enemy you killed, my friend.
I knew you in this dark; for so you frowned
Yesterday through me as you jabbed and killed.
I parried; but my hands were loath and cold.
Let us sleep now. . . .

(116–17)

This is the poet who wrote one of the most moving of all the Great War poems, "Futility." In "Strange Meeting" Owen characteristically expresses the insistent theme of tragic waste, to which has been added the vitally important theme of forgiveness and reconciliation, if only after death.

In a recent book (1989) Sybil Oldfield writes of the left-wing pacifist, Kate Courtney (1847–1929), who was a practical model of war resistance because of her rejection before and during the war of the concept of an "enemy."[11] This idea is a lesson that informs Owen's poem, and one it seems each generation has to relearn.

Poems of Protest

Catherine Marshall, addressing an audience of working women, told them:

When we think of our soldiers and sailors we think of what they suffer. . . . But we should also think of the suffering we send them forth to inflict—not from choice of theirs, but because we have found no better way. (Newberry 1977, 417–18)

Women were becoming used to hearing such strong statements by other women, and the outspokenness of much of the poetry in *Scars* is no doubt directly attributable to this change in the way women perceived themselves during the war as arbiters of moral and humane values. The poem "He Went for a Soldier" by Ruth Comfort Mitchell is one of several in the anthology that express women's bitter anger and anguish at the monstrous unnatural destructiveness of war upon those born of their bodies:

> He marched away with a blithe young score of him
>> With the first volunteers,
> Clear-eyed and clean and sound to the core of him,
>
> . . . .
> There he lies now, like a ghoulish score of him,
>> Left on the field for dead:
> The ground all around is smeared with the gore of him—
>> Even the leaves are red.
>
> . . . .
> *How much longer, O Lord, shall we bear it all?*
>> *How many more red years?*
> *Story it and glory it and share it all,*
>> *In seas of blood and tears?*
> *They are braggart attitudes we've worn so long;*
> *They are tinsel platitudes we've sworn so long—*
>> *We who have turned the Devil's Grindstone,*
>> *Borne with the hell called War!*
>
>> (*Scars*, 75–76)

This poem is one of the most explicit statements of men as cannon fodder for mother England. One of the most persistent themes in women's writing at this time was that all their nurturing had only produced young men to be killed. It was women's awareness of this senseless waste of a generation, "the tinsel platitudes" of the poem, that advanced the suffrage cause both in England and America to its inevitable conclusion. May Wright Sewall writes that at this time in America there was a very striking little cartoon on the first page of *Woman's Journal*. A woman stood and she said: "Votes for Women." "But, Madam," a soldier is supposed to be replying, "Women can't bear arms," and her answer comes, "No! Women bear armies." Sewall concludes, "Why should they [women] not have a voice then, when the question comes as to whether war or peace shall be?" (Sewall 1915, 172). The awful feeling of political powerlessness, experienced during the war by a great many women who were formerly indifferent to suffrage and other rights, provided much of the force that eventually secured women's political rights.

Still another voice of protest came from the nurses in France who had to face the actual reality of the shocking wounds the men endured. Like other young, healthy women, Mary Henderson, a VAD, no doubt felt somehow guilty in the presence of so much and such intractable pain, as her poem "An Incident" suggests:

> He was just a boy, as I could see,
> For he sat in the tent there close by me.
> I held the lamp with its flickering light,
> And felt the hot tears blur my sight
> As the doctor took the blood-stained bands
> From both his brave, shell-shattered hands—
> His boy hands, wounded more pitifully
> Than Thine, O Christ, on Calvary.
>
> .   .   .   .
> And I fed him. . . . Mary, Mother of God,
> All women tread where thy feet have trod.
>
> (Scars, 52)

Mothering is an instinct of vital importance to us all, and cannot be taken away, but the concept can perhaps be extended as suggested by the pacifist woman preacher, Maude Royden (1876–1956), who saw the world as her parish and preached that it was incumbent on us all to "mother the world." Her deepest hope was that the private, life-centred expertise of ordinary women could be adapted and applied to save the life of the world (Oldfield 1989, 65).

The idea of a shared sacrifice by patriotic means toward a divine end must have seemed comforting to the Christian women of the war years. We must remember that England was then a much more Christian country than it is today. In some ways, as the poems by some of the nurses suggest, women were as ministering angels to the wounded lost bodies and souls of men.[12] Yet how could Christian forms mitigate against the devastation, degradation, and destruction of so many young lives? In failing to condemn the evil of war, the various religious denominations betrayed Christianity itself. While some women poets identified the men's suffering with that of Christ, poets like Sassoon and Owen wrote against the empty consolations of formal religion. Sassoon's method was satire; Owen's a tragic awareness of the ironies of mortality in war and peace.

Sassoon's "They," written in October 1916, is a scathing attack on the Church of England. With unctuous rhetoric, the bishop of "They" declares that the nobility of the struggle against "Anti-Christ" will have an elevating effect on those who return: "They will not be the same."

> "We're none of us the same!" the boys reply.
> "For George lost both his legs; and Bill's stone blind;
> Poor Jim's shot through the lungs and like to die;
> And Bert's gone syphilitic: you'll not find
> A chap who's served that hasn't found *some* change."
> And the Bishop said: "The ways of God are strange!"
>
> (1925, 28)

Poets such as Owen, especially in "Dulce et Decorum Est," and Sassoon in "They" saw the terrible discrepancy between the patriotic religious sentiments and the hideous sacrifices they sanctioned and condoned. The women poets tended to identify with the sacrifice and the suffering; they did not question Christianity itself. Satire was for the men poets who could ridicule the war in all its preposterous ramifications; women, by and large, did not make fun of the war—to them it would have seemed like making fun of their menfolk. When they did use irony, it was mostly for tragic or elegiac effect rather than satiric ends, as we have seen in Macaulay's and Meynell's poetry. However, a few women did use satire, like Ruth Comfort Mitchell in her poem "He Went for a Soldier."

Although there were men and women of other religions involved in World War I in England, most people belonged to the Church of England, however nominally. Those who did belong no doubt found it difficult to escape the influence of the Church with its sense of patriotic-religious duty that was accepted in such a widespread way during the war, especially at the beginning before the first enormous casualty figures were received in the summer of 1915. Perhaps if more women had perceived how religion sanctioned the evil of war, partly by using women's age-old sense of sacrifice and Christian duty and service to others, more women might have seen militarism itself as a method of subjugating women, as oppressive in its demands on the lives of women as were Church and State.

Nurses' Poetry from the Front Line

May Sinclair's poem "Field Ambulance in Retreat" expresses the fearful anxiety and ultimate helplessness of the women who went to France to nurse the wounded and the dying: "And, where the piled corn-wagons went, our dripping / Ambulance carries home / Its red and white harvest from the fields" (*Scars*, 98). These hospitals, ambulances, trains, and tents—houses of pain and dying—are places of bitterness and despair, both for the men who suffer and die and the women who attend them, as Eva Dobell's "Night Duty" suggests:

> The pain and laughter of the day are done,
> So strangely hushed and still the long ward seems,
> Only the Sister's candle softly beams.
> Clear from the church near by the clock strikes 'one;'
> And all are wrapt away in secret sleep and dreams.
>
> .   .   .   .
> Here one cries sudden on a sobbing breath,
> Gripped in the clutch of some incarnate fear:
> What terror through the darkness draweth near?
> What memory of carnage and of death?
> What vanished scenes of dread to his closed eyes appear?
>
> And one laughs out with an exultant joy.
> An athlete he—Maybe his young limbs strain
> In some remembered game, and not in vain
> To win his side the goal—Poor crippled boy,
> Who in the waking world will never run again.
>
> (*Scars*, 32–33)

The poem captures the men's plucky cheerfulness by day, the traumatic dreams by night, and the deep psychological damage war inflicts.

The progression of the poem, from the "laughter of the day" to the hushed, candlelit ward where, watched over by a tender feminine presence, the wounded sleep in a quiet safety marked only by a nearby church clock, is suddenly shattered by a man convulsed in some nightmare vision of the battlefield. The transition from the menacing and traumatic dreams of battle to the wish fulfillment dreams of the last stanza give the poem its ironic last line. The poem makes one aware of the violence the battlefield does to men's minds as well as to their bodies.

In contrast Owen's poem "À Terre" has the line, "And grow me legs as quick as lilac-shoots." The poem begins: "Sit on the bed. I'm blind, and three parts shell. / Be careful; can't shake hands now; never shall. / Both arms have mutinied against me,—

brutes. / My fingers fidget like ten idle brats" (Blunden 1931, 87). The visual and kinetic imagery also contributes to the keen sense of actuality Owen here represents. Moreover, the poet's attitude is antiheroic: there is nothing grand or glorious about a man losing both his arms and being haunted by phantom-limb phenomena. The poem swings between tragic acceptance and anger. It certainly offers no heroic consolation.[13] Mutilation is a theme for the soldier poets as in Sassoon's "They." The vocabulary is concrete, whereas the women's vocabulary when writing of wounds, even that of the nurses who actually saw and tended these mutilations, is often abstract.

By and large women write of wounds, (wounds to be nursed with skill and pity;) but not of maiming; they do not see the men's wounds as degrading and obscene, but heroic. In other words they have not internalized the wounds as the soldier poets have. In her poem called "Pluck," Eva Dobell protests the war and its hideous appetite for men, while at the same time she invests the men's agonies and endurance with an heroic, moral dignity:

> So broke with pain, he shrinks in dread
>   To see the 'dresser' drawing near;
> And winds the clothes about his head
>   That none may see his heart-sick fear.
>   His shaking, strangled sobs you hear.
>
> But when the dreaded moment's there
>   He'll face us all, a soldier yet,
> Watch his bared wounds with unmoved air,
>   (Though tell-tale lashes still are wet),
>   And smoke his woodbine cigarette.
>
> (Scars, 31)

The first line of this poem begins, "Crippled for life at seventeen." Dobell's attitude is one of profound pity for the young soldier's devastating wounds, as well as a reverence for his endurance and suffering. There is acceptance, not anger. The poem provides yet another pieta image, as so many of the nurses' poems do. The idealized double image of maternal protection and/or maternal sacrifice is one which women like Vera Brittain in England and the artist Käthe Kollwitz in Germany would come to question closely after the war was over.[14] Both women became pacifists after the war, and both women spent the rest of their artistic lives exposing the perniciousness of the idealizing myths of war as they affected both women and men.

David Mitchell's chapter on VADs (1965) describes the shuddering and nausea of a young nurse, Enid Bagnold, as she watched the doctors re-dressing deep wounds: "Six inches deep the gauze stuck, crackling under the pull of the forceps, blood and plus leaping from the cavities." On this occasion the wounded had been lying for days between the lines in France. Mitchell goes on to say, "The emergency was so great that operations were done in the wards and amputated legs stuck in buckets in the corridors outside" (199–200).

Edith Cavell was one of the bravest of these nurses, as are the sentiments she expressed just before she was unjustifiably shot as a spy on 5 August 1915, by the Germans. "I realize that patriotism is not enough. I must have no hatred or bitterness to any one" (Hill 1915, 5). When she was arrested in a Belgian hospital, she was actually changing the bandages of a wounded German soldier.[15]

The Pieta Image: Mothers and Sons

War threatens the very maternity of women, and many of these poems express fear and despair that love cannot save, that mothering is not sufficient; it is not strong enough in the face of such savage aggression and destruction. Iris Tree's untitled poem speaks for all mourning mothers:

> Of all the tenderness that flowed to them,
> A milky way streaming from out their mother's breast,
> Stars were they to her that night, and she the stem
> From which they flowered—now barren and left unblessed.
>
> Of all the sparkling kisses that they gave
> Spangling a secret radiance on adoring hands,
> Now stifled in the darkness of a grave
> With kiss of loneliness and death's embracing bands.
>
> (Scars, 115)

If such a love could have saved them, they would not have died, the grieving poet suggests. Again we have the image of the sacrificing mother, one who finds consolation in the arms of Christianity, as the last stanza implies. As I have already suggested, the image of the pieta was a common one in women's poetry of the

First World War. It suggested passivity at a price. Although the image was unquestionably one that offered consolation (though to nonbelievers and women of other faiths it may have been an empty consolation), at the same time it prevented women from questioning the politicization of their supposed idealized role. Poetically, the pieta image seemed an essential component of women's consciousness.

One of the chief ideas that the pacifist women kept emphasizing and challenging was the idea that hate must always rule. In speaking to an assembly of women at the Kingsway Hall in London on 13 May 1915, just after The Hague conference, Helena Swanwick, the chairwoman, spoke of the theme of "the unchangeableness of human nature" as being an old one. It is, she asserts, the hoariest of lies. "We *can* change if we *will* change," she exclaimed. "And *this* is one of the ideas we are changing, we women—this idea that hate must always rule" (Swanwick 1915, 20). But the fight against the hatred that was a powerful element in the war mentality was not easy, as Dobell's poem, "Son of Mine," dedicated to all pacifist mothers, clearly states:

> He stood erect to make his claim
>   Before his judges, life and truth
> Shone in his eyes, steadfast and sane,
>   With all the fire of candid youth.
>
> The questioning began, he said
>   That warfare was a crime to him
> Unpardonable—that it led
>   To worse than loss of life or limb.
>
> . . . .
> For base defusions—vain, untrue,
>   The stern-faced men presiding jeered
> "Come, we can't stop all day with you!":
>   The others by him yawned and sneered.
>
>   (Dobell 1915)

The young man is sent to prison, put into "convict's garb," given prison food, not allowed to see the sky; he dies a sudden death. The tribunals that heard the cases of young men like Dobell had actually been set up by the Derby scheme to secure men for the army. It is not surprising that they found it difficult to change their approach. The men on these tribunals had little sympathy with the socialist or religious beliefs of most pacifists. The eight or nine men that composed each of the two thousand tribunals set up by March 1916 were elderly former civil servants, policemen, and clergymen, most of them middle class—all devoted to their country and its war effort (Moorehead 1987, 31).

Jingoistic Poetry

Catherine Reilly remarks that white-feather poetry appeared regularly in newspapers and periodicals of the day.[16] Jessie Pope was one of these strident propagandists for victory and national glory, no matter what the cost, as in these verses from "The Call":

> Who's for the trench—
>   Are you, my laddie?
> Who'll follow French—
>   Will you, my laddie?
> Who's fretting to begin,
> Who's going out to win?
> And who wants to save his skin—
>   Do you, my laddie?
>
> Who's for the khaki suit—
>   Are you, my laddie?
> Who longs to charge and shoot—
>   Do you, my laddie?
> Who's keen on getting fit,
> Who means to show his grit,
> And who'd rather wait a bit—
>   Would you, my laddie?
>
> Who'll earn the Empire's thanks—
>   Will you, my laddie?
> Who'll swell the victor's ranks—
>   Will you, my laddie?
> When that procession comes,
> Banners and rolling drums—
> Who'll stand and bite his thumbs—
>   Will you, my laddie?

(Scars, 88)

The disturbing mixture of playfulness and threat, portraying war as a game for young boys to glory in, no doubt had its appeal to some. The voices of the jingoistic women urged the men on to fight dutifully and honorably for a Christian England and a

rightful cause regardless of the carnage. In response to such attitudes Wilfred Owen dedicated one of his most savage antiwar
poems to "a certain Poetess"; she was Jessie Pope. Much anthologized, "Dulce et Decorum Est" is what Owen called "a gas
poem."[17] The last stanza reads:

> If in some smothering dreams, you too could pace
> Behind the wagon that we flung him in,
> And watch the white eyes writhing in his face,
> His hanging face, like a devil's sick of sin;
> If you could hear, at every jolt, the blood
> Come gargling from the froth-corrupted lungs,
> Bitter as the cud
> Of vile, incurable sores on innocent tongues,—
> My friend, you would not tell with such high zest
> To children ardent for some desperate glory,
> The old Lie: Dulce et decorum est
> Pro patria mori.

> (Owen 1931, 66)

Owen's purpose is to shock the overzealous patriots into a
realistic vision of the actual suffering experienced by the men
who sign up. It is a plea to women like Jessie Pope and those
she influenced to reconsider the terrible discrepancy between
their jingoism and the obscenities it sanctioned. Owen's "Anthem for Doomed Youth" and Sassoon's "Wirers" and "Working
Party" are other poems that give the lie to Jessie Pope's perception of the war.

In *Jus Suffragii*, the international suffrage newspaper published in Geneva, Mary Sheepshanks wrote a bitter editorial de-
ploring jingoism such as that of Jessie Pope. It was not enough
for women to do relief work, she warned; they must use their
brains to urge a peace-creating climate of opinion and not a
vengeful one.

S. Gertrude Ford's "A Fight to a Finish" answers the jingoistic
patriotic voices of the motherland in angry tones:

> 'Fight the year out!' the War-lords said:
> What said the dying among the dead?

> 'To the last man!' cried the profiteers:
> What said the poor in the starveling years?
> 'War is good!' yelled the Jingo-kind:
> What said the wounded, the maimed and blind?

'Fight on!' the Armament-kings besought:
Nobody asked what the women thought.

(Scars, 38)

This is one of the most political and satirical poems in the anthology (together with Gertrude Ford's other poem, "The Tenth Armistice Day"). Despite the paucity of such poems, many women thought similarly: that to prevent anything like this war from ever happening again, they needed the vote. More and more women who until now had not been interested in political rights joined with the suffragist women, both pacifists and activists, in their realization that if their voices were to be heard by those who legislate war, they had to have the vote behind them.

The Munitions Workers

While some women were protesting the war and others were glorifying it, still others expressed a sense of guilty despair at women's working role, as in Ida Bedford's "Munition Wages":

> I've bracelets and jewellery,
>   Rings envied by friends;
> A sergeant to swank with,
>   And something to lend.
>
> I drive out in taxis,
>   Do theatres in style.
> And this is mi verdict
>   It is jolly worth while.

(Scars, 7)

There is exasperation here for the girl's wild extravagance, but also implicit approval for a newfound independence and purposiveness. Most of the girls who worked in the munitions factories were from the working classes and were happy to be released from the bondage of domestic service which imprisoned most of them before the war. They worked a twelve-hour shift in the factories, six days a week, and spent their hard-earned money much faster than they had earned it, but we can hazard a guess that they were more contented than in their prewar jobs. David Mitchell (1965) writes that when they were demobilized the girls wept at the ending of what they now saw as the happiest, most purposeful days of their lives. It would seldom, if ever, occur to

them that their purposefulness brought violent death not only
to the enemy but to some of their own menfolk, too.

The Poetry of "Them" and "Us"

Yet another female voice is that which expresses anger and
dismay at the frivolity and coquettishness of some women, in
spite of the war. Edith Sitwell's poem, "The Dancers," subtitled
"During a Great Battle, 1916," is an example:

> The floors are slippery with blood:
> The world gyrates too. God is good
> That while His wind blows out the light
> For those who hourly die for us—
> We still can dance, each night.
>
> The music has grown numb with death—
> But we will suck their dying breath,
> The whispered name they breathed to chance,
> To swell our music, make it loud
> That we may dance,—may dance.
>
> We are the dull blind carrion-fly
> That dance and batten. Though God die
> Mad from the horror of the light—
> The light is mad, too, flecked with blood,—
> We dance, we dance, each night.
>
> (Scars, 100)

The poem is in keeping with the received wisdom that the
men are dying for the women and that some of the women seem
not to care. One wonders who these women were. The patriotic
jingo-types who saw dying for the glory of England as a Christian
duty to be rewarded in heaven? But, Sitwell suggests, even God
may die with horror at such human wickedness, even though He
takes the spirit of the dead men away and allows their womenfolk
to dance. The distasteful image of "sucking their dying breath"
carries over to that of the "carrion-fly," suggesting that the dancers (perhaps men and women) are like predators, battening on
the blood of the brave men in France and symbolically dancing
on it—on the floors that are slippery with its stickiness. The
many associations behind the medieval symbol of the dance of

death add a rich expansiveness to the poem, as does the symbolic significance of Christ as the light of the world. The poem's mood is one of protest and rejection, especially of the division between those at home who can still dance and the men at the front who writhe in agonies of mutilation, sacrificing their lives for the frivolous, complacent "dancers" who make a mockery of their sufferings. There is a sense that everything is unbalanced, the men's fate and the dancers' movements partake of a similar frenzied madness: "the world gyrates too."

This division that Sitwell and other women write of—between those who stayed at home and talked of war and those who went to the front, fought and suffered—is an important theme for the soldier poets too. The soldiers wrote of two divisions: that between themselves and the staff officers who remained behind the lines at base headquarters, giving inept commands that resulted in the sacrifice of men's lives; and between themselves and those who remained at home, both men and women, who seemed indifferent to their cause.

Sassoon's poem "Base Details" focuses on the general staff and its gross physical, moral and imaginative remove from the world of the troops:

> If I were fierce and bald and short of breath,
>   I'd live with scarlet Majors at the Base,
> And speed glum heroes up the line to death.
>   You'd see me with my puffy petulant face,
> Guzzling and gulping in the best hotel,
>   Reading the Roll of Honour. "Poor young chap,"
> I'd say—"I used to know his father well;
>   Yes, we've lost heavily in this last scrap."
> And when the war is done and youth stone dead,
> I'd toddle safely home and die—in bed.
>
> (*Selected Poems* 1925, 29)

And in "Suicide in the Trenches" Sassoon wrathfully lashes out at civilian ignorance:

> You smug-faced crowds with kindling eye
> Who cheer when soldier lads march by,
> Sneak home and pray you'll never know
> The hell where youth and laughter go.
>
> (ibid., 39)

In "Glory of Women" the poet directs his scorn at some women's shallowness and ingenuousness and their inclination to accept the falsities of the romantic interpretation of war:

> You love us when we're heroes, home on leave,
> Or wounded in a mentionable place.
> You worship decorations; you believe
> That chivalry redeems the war's disgrace

(ibid., 42)

The attack seems immoderate and indiscriminatory; but no doubt the rage was irresistible. Moreover, as the war went on, the injustice of it grew in the minds of the men at the front, and the writers tended to magnify aspects of the undeniable disparity between the sacrifices demanded of soldiers and those demanded of civilians. Both "Suicide in the Trenches" and "Glory of Women" appeared in *Counter-Attack*, Sassoon's volume of war poems published in July 1918. *Counter-Attack* represented an uncompromising rejection of all the war had come to signify. Most of the women writers represented in *Scars* would have read it with horrified sympathy and appalled understanding.

The poems in *Scars Upon My Heart* vary a good deal in form and skill, but they are pervaded by horror of war, and an immense admiration and gratitude to the men. The anthology is a narrative record of women's consciousness at a crucial time in history, and if women could not actively share the battleground, they shared its results: the annihilation of husbands, sons, lovers, brothers, and friends.

Poems of Grief and Mourning

To my mind the most moving of the poems are those that mourn the dead. The grief is both personal and universal. The poets speak ironically of the fertility of Mother Nature in England and the sterility of the would-be mothers, as in Sara Teasdale's "Spring in War-Time": "I feel the Spring far off, far off, / The faint far scent of bud and leaf— / Oh how can Spring take heart to come / To a world in grief, / Deep grief?" (*Scars*, 110). The same elegiac tone and control characterize Olive Lindsay's poem "Despair": "Half of me died at Bapaume, / And the rest of me is a log" (*Scars*, 64). There is the same inconsolable sadness in loss in Margaret Postgate Cole's "Afterwards":

Oh, my beloved, shall you and I
Ever be young again, be young again?
The people that were resigned said to me
—Peace will come and you will lie
Under the larches up in Sheer,

. . . .

And peace came. And lying in Sheer
I look round at the corpses of the larches
Whom they slew to make pit-props
For mining the coal for the great armies.
And think, a pit-prop cannot move in the wind,
Nor have red manes hanging in spring from its branches,
And sap making the warm air sweet.

. . . .

And if these years have made you into a pit-prop,
To carry the twisting galleries of the world's reconstruction

. . . .

What use is it to you? What use
To have your body lying here
In Sheer, underneath the larches?

(Scars, 21–22)

Here the dead loved one has become one with nature, but it is
a nature viewed as inert—like the dead tree, its sap dried up,
cut and fashioned into a "pit-prop" to support subsequent
aboveground redevelopment. The theme of war as a violent
means for violent ends—and its ultimate futility—is suggested
in the analogy between the larches which "they slew" and now
look like "corpses" and the soldiers themselves. The "twisting
galleries" suggest not only the passages of underground coal
mines, but also the trenches themselves, those man-made con-
structions that received and dealt death to millions. Furthermore, because of the labyrinthine structure of the trenches, fire
was an ever present hazard. Some trenches were used as mass
graves, and the image of the dead men holding up what is left
of civilization they died for is as haunting as it is tragic.
    It is interesting to compare Owen's poem "Miners" with Cole's
"Afterwards." The Royal Sappers and Miners was the former title
of the Royal Engineers, and Owen would have been familiar with
these miner-soldiers who were responsible for maintaining the
structural strength of the trench roofs, as well as for making tun-
nels under no-man's-land so as to set off explosions behind the

German lines.[18] Both Postgate's poem and Owen's make an exceptional connection, both use the same imagery, and both poets put soldiers and miners into the same category; all of them die, Owen writes, so that:

> The centuries will burn rich loads
>   With which we groaned,
> Whose warmth shall lull their dreaming lids
>   While songs are crooned.
> But they will not dream of us poor lads
>   Lost in the ground.
>
> (H. Gardner 1972, 902)

As the war with its appalling inhuman conditions went on and on and the casualty lists grew stupefyingly long, there was a mounting desperation in place of any kind of enthusiasm. However, it was impossible to any great extent to question the men's sacrifice itself; they were courageous and dutiful, their lives were being wasted in a gross, obscene folly. The collective narrative of *Scars Upon My Heart* reaches its conclusion in a mood of quiet if bitter reconciliation: survival itself must be survived; it is women's burden and privilege to care for a new generation built out of the never-to-be-forgotten action of that "lost generation" whose wounds, both physical and spiritual, have scarred the women's hearts forever. In Vera Brittain's words, addressed in 1915 to her beloved brother just before his death:

> Your battle-wounds are scars upon my heart,
>   Received when in that grand and tragic 'show'
> You played your part
>   Two years ago, . . .
>
> (*Scars*, 15)

When she wrote these painful words, she little realized she was yet to endure the cruel death of her beloved fiancé, Roland, in 1918. This heartfelt identification of the women with the men at the front is the true answer to Sassoon. Another response came from those women writers who seemed to think of the war in abstract terms, as a force their men were horribly subject to, but not responsible for; as a result these women separated the men's actions and sufferings from the war machine itself, organized as it was by the patriarchal military structure. Other, more politically aware women, especially the pacifists among them, recognized the overwhelming influence of patriarchy in the waging of the war. The soldier poets did not seem to separate the human perpetrators and victims of warfare; however, they did come to blame bitterly the military hierarchy for the continuation of the war, as Sassoon's poem "Base Details" shows so clearly.

Poems of the Final Year, 1918

Charlotte Mew's poem "The Cenotaph" (actually dated September 1919) speaks of the loneliness, the heartache, and the sorrow women felt in 1918, but it also speaks of a spirit dedicated to the renewal of life painfully won for the Allies on the fields of France:

Not yet will those measureless fields be green again
Where only yesterday the wild sweet blood of wonderful youth
          was shed;
There is a grave whose earth must hold too long, too deep a
          stain,
Though for ever over it we may speak as proudly as we may
          tread.
But here, where the watchers by lonely hearths from the thrust
          of an inward sword have more slowly bled,
We shall build the Cenotaph: Victory, winged, with Peace,
          winged too, at the column's head.
And over the stairway, at the foot—oh! here, leave desolate,
          passionate hands to spread
Violets, roses, and laurel, with the small, sweet, twinkling
          country things
Speaking so wistfully of other Springs,
From the little gardens of little places where son or sweetheart
          was born and bred.
In splendid sleep, with a thousand brothers
                    To lovers—to mothers,
                    Here, too, lies he:
Under the purple, the green, the red,
It is all young life: it must break some women's hearts to see
Such a brave, gay coverlet to such a bed!
Only, when all is done and said,
God is not mocked and neither are the dead. . . .

                                        (Scars, 71)

The poem suggests that women's deep anguished grief must take solace in the Christian virtues of forgiveness and reconciliation, and that they must find the courage to live on without their loved

ones in the service of the world. The best salvation was work
and reparation, as Mew's earlier poem, written in 1915, suggests:

> Let us remember Spring will come again
>> To the scorched, blackened woods, where the
>> wounded trees
> Wait with their old wise patience for the heavenly rain,
> Sure of the sky: sure of the sea to send its healing breeze,
> Sure of the sun. And even as to these
>> Surely the Spring, when God shall please,
> Will come again like a divine surprise
> To those who sit today with their great Dead, hands in their
> hands, eyes in their eyes,
> At one with Love, at one with Grief: blind to the scattered things
> and changing skies.
>
> (*Scars*, 72)

Unlike most of the soldier poets, (especially Owen and Sassoon), most women seemed to find comfort in the belief that God
would heal the wounds of war; they did not seem as aware of
the terrible discrepancy between the patriotic-religious elegiac
attitude and the sacrifices that it sanctioned and commemorated.
The magnitude of those sacrifices caused Charles Sorley to reject
all elegiac sentiments, "Say only this, 'They are dead.'" In "Anthem for Doomed Youth" Owen, on the other hand, balances the
consolatory rituals of Christian burial against the degradation of
those "who die as cattle":

> What passing-bells for these who die as cattle?
>> Only the monstrous anger of the guns.
>> Only the stuttering rifles' rapid rattle
> Can patter out their hasty orisons.
> No mockeries for them from prayers or bells,
>> Nor any voice of mourning save the choirs,—
> The shrill, demented choirs of wailing shells;
>> And bugles calling for them from sad shires.
>
> (1931, 80)

For women poets like Charlotte Mew and Mary Anderson and
the women they spoke for, the interpretation of the war in Christian terms mitigated their grief and allowed them a reconciliation
with the men's fate that the men themselves rejected. Perhaps
men were burdened with a sense of responsibility for the war
that women without political rights could not, and indeed
should not, share. The women had been plunged into a disas-

trous war through no fault of theirs. But what religious formali-
ties can encompass the enormity of life and death in modern
warfare? The Christian Church of England had betrayed itself
since it failed to condemn the war; moreover, it had ignored one
of Christ's most important commands and implicitly sanctioned
murderous violence. The soldier poets were not about to sanctify
such evil.

In the poem addressed to her small son, Tony, aged three, Marjorie Wilson speaks for the thousands of bereaved women left
with the peacetime task of bringing up a new generation, alone:

> And when across the peaceful English land,
> Unhurt by war, the light is growing dim,
>   And you remember by your shadowed bed
> All those—the brave—you must remember him.
>
>   And know it was for you who bear his name,
> And such as you that all his joy he gave—
>   His love of quiet fields, his youth, his life,
> To win that heritage of peace you have.

> (*Scars*, 130)

Again the elegiac mood and theme support the need to forgive
the hideousness of the war, but also expressed is the need not
to forget. Although the English land is at peace, "unhurt," shadows pass over it, invisible presences of all those who died, whose
spirits watch over their children. The children in turn must be
brought up to love the "quiet fields" and "that heritage" their
father's sacrifice secured for them. It is sobering to think that the
little boy addressed in this poem would have been twenty when
World War II began.

S. Gertrude Ford's poem "The Tenth Armistice Day" makes
the necessary political point: "'Lest we forget!' Let us remember,
then, / . . . They warred to end war: to fulfil their hope / Give
them a better monument and fitter; / Build their memorial in
the League of Nations!" (*Scars*, 39). And Eleanor Farjeon's poem
"Peace" makes the vitally important moral point that we must
be ever vigilant in keeping the peace—but not by preparing for
war: "Be blunt, and say that peace is but a state / Wherein the
active soul is free to move, / And nations only show as mean or
great / According to the spirit then they prove.—/ O which of ye
whose battle-cry is Hate / Will first in peace dare shout the name
of Love?" (*Scars*, 37). The poem grimly personifies peace and
war as brothers, Janus-faced, reminding one of the politician's

phrase, "keeping the peace by preparing for war." The poem also elaborates the familiar metaphor of war as a monster that devours fathers and sons, ironically supporting the theme of the dualism of war and peace by suggesting that in peace we fatten and nourish our loved ones only to feed this monster. These poems encourage a reader like myself to ask: are love and hate, peace and war, really opposite sides of the same coin, the same body? In human relationships it is sometimes difficult to perceive where love stops and hate begins, so intermingled can these basic feelings be; but in the moral and political life of a nation and an individual, it should be possible to separate this Janus-figure, if we use judgment before we act—judgment based on love of permanent peace. Most probably it is only education that will really change those attitudes that need changing. We could start with our children.

The sentimentality of many of the poems in Scars Upon My Heart suggests the pressures on women who, wanting to protest the war, nevertheless wanted to remain appropriately feminine. Yet it is fair to say that the poems as a collection still manage implicitly to constitute a critique of both nationalism and patriarchal culture. The fact that it was not until 1981 that Catherine Reilly collected and published them as a single narrative of multiple feminine voices, supports the view that what was most conspicuously missing in the twenties was the means whereby women could speak with one voice to define, describe, and validate their war experience. As the reader will notice from excerpts in the previous chapter, women's prose is stronger and more direct than many of the poems in Scars. But one must consider the different audiences the writers had in mind, as well as their intentions. Writers such as the Pankhursts, Emily Hobhouse, Evelyn Keys, and Helena Swanwick were used to speaking in public, urging women to fight for the vote and then the war effort, or the antiwar effort. Most of the poets in Scars reflect women's consciousness at a momentous time in history, registering anguished endurance, not defiant militarism. Writing and responding to poetry are private reflective activities; especially is this true of individual poems published in daily newspapers as many the poems in Scars were. Furthermore, masculine attitudes toward women who wrote about the Great War were, at best, skeptical. During 1914–18 war was still perceived by the majority of women and men as heroic and essentially masculine.

3

Women between the World Wars, 1918–1939

As we have seen, before British women got the vote in 1918 they were politically impotent to legislate for peace; after they got the vote and World War I was over, what did they do to help prevent the Second World War? Women like the experienced suffragist pacifist Helena Swanwick knew that "nothing would come of pacifism that refused hard political thought and relied solely on emotion" (Swanwick 1935, 343). Furthermore, how did winning the franchise improve the rights of women? What did women do with their vote?

Political Women in Britain, 1918–1939

In 1918 in the first general election in which women could vote, 1,623 candidates contested 707 parliamentary seats. Only seventeen, or hardly more than one percent, of these candidates were women. Four women stood as Labour candidates, a surprisingly low figure since Labour had been the party traditionally associated with support for the suffrage movement.[1] Three of these women, Mrs. Pethick Lawrence, Mrs. Charlotte Despard, and Mrs. H. M. MacKenzie, had been well-known suffragists.

During the latter part of World War I pacifist suffrage leaders such as Helena Swanwick and Catherine Marshall advocated a Women's Party so that women's concerns could be represented directly and thus there would be no compromise with party politics and no sell-out by male politicians. Immediately after the split between the pacifist and militant suffragists in the early spring of 1915, Catherine Marshall sent Helena Swanwick an outline for a Women's Independent Party, "An organization that should stand for *real* democracy, *real* feminism, *real* internationalism" (quoted in Wiltsher 1985, 73).

In any case the militant suffragists were also in favor of a Women's Party, and in the general election of 1918 Christabel Pankhurst stood as representative of the Women's Party, which grew directly out of the Women's Social and Political Union (WSPU). But the Women's Party never caught the political awareness of most women, meeting instead with suspicion and only mixed suppport among women. Moreover, it was perceived to be the continuation of the militant feminism which many men— and a significant number of M.P.s—had always feared.[2]

Eight other women who stood at this election were independents of one kind and another. Only one woman was elected, Countess Markiewicz (1868–1927), who campaigned from prison. An Irishwoman married to a Polish aristocrat, she was elected as Sinn Fein member for St. Patrick's division, Dublin, but she did not take her seat in the House of Commons, as a protest against British policy on Ireland.

Although the suffragists had won the franchise, they had not won the confidence of enough women and men voters that they should be in the government. In other words, women had won the right to vote, not the right to govern; to be represented but not to make policy.

After the enormous effort and sacrifice that went into the achievement of the Emancipation Act of 7 December 1917, one would have thought that taking their seats in Parliament would be a logical extension of the long and arduous fight for women's rights that the suffragists had won. One would not only expect more women standing as candidates than there were, but also more women voting for women candidates. However, the long battle to obtain the vote apparently did not develop in women this parliamentary political consciousness. Some commentators suggest that the struggle for the vote was at bottom a nonparty political activity. Getting the vote, however, was not an end in itself in the minds of most women, but a new beginning. As the 1918 election demonstrated, new beginnings can be troubled.

Ironically the first woman to take her seat in Parliament was neither a political activist nor a suffragist—that may in fact be why she was elected at the by-election for Plymouth in November 1919. She inherited the constituency, truly speaking, from her husband, who had been elevated to the House of Lords. She was neither middle class, dedicated, nor politically and socially radical; what is more she was very rich and American-born. The only woman member of Parliament from 1919 to 1921 Lady Astor did not represent much of a threat to the male bastion of the House of Commons. Although she maintained her Conservative seat until 1945, she never gained cabinet rank. In 1921 Mrs. Wintringham, whose husband, Tom Wintringham, had died, took over his seat in the House, and so she joined Lady Astor as the second woman to sit in the House. Even after 1921 the number of British women parliamentarians between the wars was precious few, as the following figures show: 1922, 8 (number standing 33); 1923, 8 (number standing 34); 1924, 4 (number standing 41); 1929, 14 (number standing 69); 1931, 15 (number standing 62); 1935, 9 (number standing 67) *(Times Guide to the House of Commons)*. At the outbreak of the Second World War there were twelve women members of Parliament, and none held cabinet rank.

The general election of 1922 produced no new woman member of Parliament, although thirty-three women stood. In May 1923 Mrs. Hilton Philipson was elected when her husband was debarred from standing for Parliament because of some improper practices of his political agent. Thus in 1923 all three women members had taken over seats already held by their husbands; it is unlikely that this was a mere coincidence. Getting used to the idea of women as political representatives was of course very new. Perhaps most people, women and men, feared that these new feminist politicians would be too radical and iconoclastic. Yet the three women in Parliament had not been self-assertive and had not sought a place in the House for themselves per se but rather to help out their husbands. They were not essentially political women, but helpful, politically supportive wives. Their candidacy was perhaps seen by their constituents as an extension of their roles as wives and even mothers. What is more, their husbands had already politicized their role for them. Not only did they take over the standing and legitimacy of their husbands, but they inherited safe seats. Most of the other women who stood for Parliament in these early years struggled with enormous difficulties such as obtaining Party political support, being of unknown backgrounds, and standing for unwinnable or at very best marginal seats. The combination of winnable seats and male acceptance that these first three women M. P.s were given, without much effort on their parts, partly explains how they—and not the committed feminists—were the first to achieve political honors.[3]

Women very much needed educating in political and party candidacy and electioneering. But postwar pressures on women to enjoy being housewives prevented the necessary political activity. What working-class women were getting instead was training by government agencies in various kinds of domesticity such as "Mother Care" and "Homecare." A journalist writing in 1920 in a woman's magazine leaves us in no doubt about the way things were supposed to go for women:

> The tide of progress which leaves woman with the vote in her hand and scarcely any clothes upon her back is ebbing, and the sex is returning to the deep, very deep sea of feminity from which her newly-acquired power can be more effectively wielded.[4]

Although middle-class women had more job opportunities, they also were subject to the prevailing propaganda that women's place was in the home. The approved image of women of all classes at this time was as wives and mothers of workers. The average woman was not supposed to be interested in politics. In the all-out effort to reelect Labour M.P.s in 1923, housewives were told "the proudest of housewives can afford to let her housework slide a little for the weeks of the general election."[5]

In Britain, 1929 was the year of the so-called Flapper Election. Now that everyone over twenty-one could vote, it was hoped women would be more of a force in getting women into Parliament: about seven million new female voters were added to the electoral roll. But of the sixty-nine women who stood for election (compared with forty-one in 1924), only fourteen were elected (Brookes 1967, 71–84). It might be interesting to put these figures into the international context: in 1926 there were three women in the United States Congress and six women in the Austrian parliament, but thirty-two women in the Reichstag. In 1929, women made up 1.1 percent of the membership of the U. S. Congress, 2.1 percent of the House of Commons, and 6.7 percent of the Reichstag. In March 1933, there were fifteen women Members of Parliament in Britain and thirty women deputies in the Reichstag. To these figures one must add the astonishing fact that women in France, Spain, Italy, and Switzerland had yet to be enfranchised.[6] (We shall return later to the fact that by November 1933 there were no women in the Reichstag.) The general election of 1935 in Britain was the last until after the war, and it was therefore perhaps unfortunate for women that the Parliament included so few of them. Of the nine women returned, six were Conservatives, one Labour, one Liberal, and one Independent.

Throughout this period leading up to World War II these women M.P.s were actively engaged in the debate on appeasement. In 1937 Ellen Wilkinson was calling for the formation of a popular front with the Communists and the ILP, but this was rejected by the rest of the executives of the Labour Party. In 1938 Eleanor Rathbone published her book *War Can Be Averted* in which she argued that this would only be the case were the members of the League of Nations prepared to stand up to aggression, if necessary by limited action "not only within the League as a whole, but within the States whose co-operation may reasonably be expected, the arms and the men for successful resistance are there, if there is will to use them" (Rathbone 1938, 17). Also in 1938 the Duchess of Atholl, who had been in Parliament since 1923, espoused the cause of Republican Spain, and as a direct result of this action her constituency party decided to seek a new candidate.

After Munich and the development of a full-blown appeasement policy, the House became completely divided in support for either Chamberlain or Churchill, and the by-election which the Duchess decided to fight in the winter of 1938 became symbolic of the wider issues of war and peace. There were only two candidates: the Duchess, a supporter of Churchill, and the official new Conservative candidate, a supporter of Chamberlain. For the last time appeasement won, and the Duchess lost her seat (Brookes 1967, 127).

Many reasons continue to be given—even today in the 1990s—as to why so few women have succeeded in getting into Parliament, from the domestic—it is difficult to leave families and live at Westminster when the House is sitting—to the intellectual—that most women who do succeed do not want to be thought of as women politicians per se, but as politicians. There is a continuing false assumption that women will vote for women candidates because they are women; female politicians need to band together to educate women about voting for them and thus having an appropriate voice in Parliament. It is an outdated perception to think women will always be interested only in women's issues such as health, welfare, education, family and matrimonial affairs, although historically these are the areas of concern women parliamentarians have been relegated to. They are, of course, areas of concern that draw on women's practical skills.

However, what is wanted as well is and was for women to be active in foreign and international affairs and the economy.

So much then for women parliamentarians between the wars; there should have been more of them, especially in foreign affairs. Internationalism is surely an eminently feminist ideal which, given the chance, women can work for with courage, imagination, and success. Ideally, the prewar female electorate should have been made more aware of the role they could have played. But that awareness would have had to have been a powerful one as far back as 1935 when the last general election before the war was called.

So to answer one of the opening questions of this chapter—what did women do with their vote once they had it?—the answer seems to be that the mass of women in Britain and, as we shall see, to a lesser extent in Germany gave their vote to men candidates, if they voted at all. What equality for women meant in the period between the two world wars remained a question of ideological significance for women in their still subordinate economic, social, and sexual roles. It is difficult to obtain figures of just how many women in Britain did vote in the parliamentary elections from 1919 to 1939. It is certainly true that at no time during this period were there ever enough women in any Parliament.

On this vital issue of women in Parliament, perhaps we can anticipate by jumping forty years. Even in the 1980s there was little sign of real progress in the number of women in Parliament. The remarkable fact is that the number of women elected to Parliament in Great Britain in 1983 was twenty-three out of a House of 650, that is, a mere 3.5 percent. The next astonishing fact is that 52 percent of the electorate at that time was female. Yes, Britain has had a female Prime Minister, but when Margaret Thatcher reached the top in 1979 she was one of only 19 women M.P.s among 616 males.

It is the lack of women in the House that has led Lesley Abdela to found a national organization called the 300 Group for Women in Politics and Public Life. The ambitious aim of the group to see half the House of Commons female seems increasingly realistic. Whereas there were only nineteen in 1979, and twenty-three in 1983, there were in 1992 sixty women M.P.s—a record number, three times more than there were twenty years earlier.

Furthermore, immediately after the 1992 election, the prime minister, John Major, appointed his first cabinet and included Virginia Bottomley as Health Secretary and Gillian Shephard as

Employment Secretary. This move countered widespread criticism of Major when he failed to appoint a single woman in his first cabinet sixteen months earlier. *The Times Guide to the House of Commons* in 1992 was positively enthusiastic: "Some campaigners for equal representation now feel that a realistic target would be 100 women M.P.s by the end of the decade. Failure to achieve this will not be due to any lack of enthusiasm. The 1992 election set new records for women, both in terms of candidates standing and members elected. The 1987 election was hailed as a breakthrough for exactly the same reasons" (282).

British Women's Pacifist and Political Groups, 1919–1939

After the First World War was over several nonpartisan women's groups formed to promote the cause of peace and the rights of women. The Women's International League for Peace and Freedom (WILPF), which developed out of The Hague International Women's Congress of 1915 (see chapter 1), was one of the influential women's organizations that sought continuously between the two world wars to establish conditions for a just and durable peace. The WILPF was concerned with social and political issues, objective fact-finding, and the formulation of just and humane policies. The group worked in two directions, through its national sections bringing pressure on respective governments and through its international office in Geneva making direct approaches to delegates at the new League of Nations, formed in 1920. The national sections published their own bulletins, and Geneva published an international newsletter, *Jus Suffragii* (Bussey and Tims 1980, 25–33).

The first elected president of WILPF (1915) was Jane Addams, the much admired American social philosopher and reformer, who in 1931 was awarded the Nobel Prize for Peace for her work with WILPF. The two vice presidents, both very well known activists and pacifists, were Helena Swanwick from Britain and Gustava Heymann from Germany. Emily Balch, whose professorship at Wellesley College had been terminated in 1918 after twenty-five years, in part because of her pacifist activities, was the first international secretary at Geneva.

The first annual international Congress of WILPF after the war was held in Zurich in May 1919. This time the British government did not prevent British women from attending, and twenty-five of them were present as well as women from other countries such as France, Norway, U. S., and Germany. Among the German contingent was the young Gertrude Baer of Munich, who was later to have her writings confiscated and be forced out of Germany by the Nazis.

The conference gave the women gathered in Zurich an opportunity to consider the Versailles Treaty. Tims writes that their reaction to it was an overwhelming indictment of its terms:

> This International Congress of Women expresses its deep regret that the terms of peace proposed at Versailles should so seriously violate the principles upon which alone a just and lasting peace can be secured, and which the democracies of the world had come to accept.
>
> By guaranteeing the fruits of the secret treaties to the conquerors, the terms of peace tacitly sanction secret diplomacy, deny the principles of self-determination, recognize the rights of the victors to the spoils of war, and create all over Europe discords and animosities which can only lead to future wars.
>
> By the demand for the disarmament of one set of belligerents only, the principle of justice is violated and the rule of force is continued.
>
> By the financial and economic proposals a hundred million people of this generation in the heart of Europe are condemned to poverty, disease and despair, which must result in the spread of hatred and anarchy within each nation.
>
> With a deep sense of responsibility, this Congress strongly urges the Allied and Associated Governments to accept such amendments of the terms as shall bring the peace into harmony with those principles first enumerated by President Wilson, upon the faithful carrying out of which the honour of the Allied peoples depends. (Bussey and Tims 1980, 31)

None of the women's proposals was accepted by the Big Four, and only President Wilson troubled to acknowledge them; nevertheless, with the formation of the new League of Nations WILPF concentrated on making the League a significant force for peace.

At their own conferences and meetings both national and international, the women of WILPF were by now used to speaking and being heard. But in the new League of Nations the women's voices were vastly outnumbered and consequently swallowed up by the male majority. Nevertheless, on 2 December 1920, Emily Balch sent to every delegate at the first assembly a copy of The Hague and Zurich resolutions together with proposals for necessary steps to be taken by the League:

1. To admit without delay all nations expressing their desire to be admitted and their willingness to perform the duties of members.
2. To amend the Covenant so as to make both Council and Assembly more directly representative of the peoples, so that they may command the confidence of the world as really international and impartial bodies.
3. To begin, as soon as possible, a general and effective reduction of armaments, as a first step towards the elimination from international relations of the use and threat of force.
4. To adopt the fullest possible publicity for the proceedings of the Council and the Assembly, in order to enlighten public opinion and win public confidence (Bussey and Tims 36).

During this first assembly WILPF also sent a number of special memoranda to every delegation. Two of these documents were printed verbatim in the League's official journal, the first dealing with the use by the League of the weapon of blockade, against which strong arguments were made; the second dealing with the use of violence and terror—an all too common feature of the postwar world, in spite of the theoretical protection of minorities against atrocities provided for in the minorities treaties.

All this activity on the part of WILPF took place in the first months of the first assembly of the League of Nations. According to Bussey and Tims, close and friendly relations were established with many of the delegates and permanent officials, but this did not blind WILPF to the defects of the new organization. The disarmament clauses of the Versailles Treaty (whereby Germany alone was kept disarmed, albeit *pour encourager les autres*) had been amongst the most contentious. From the beginning, the WILPF insisted that only total and universal disarmament could be effective. The WILPF also perceived that internal as well as international disarmament was an essential condition of peace. In the thirties Austria, Germany, Hungary, Italy, Bulgaria, and Romania all had illegal armed organizations, which the League of Nations could do nothing about since domestic affairs were not within its jurisdiction.

The WILPF had not been established as a pacifist organization per se, in the simple sense of adherence to the principle of nonresistance. At the third international WILPF congress in Vienna in 1922, a motion that the organization "adopt the principle and practice of Non-Resistance under all circumstances" received a simple majority vote but was ruled not binding upon national sections. Even in 1919, there had been divergences of opinion on the attitude the emerging League of Nations should take to the movements of violent revolution in Europe. Military interventions by western governments against revolutionary regimes in Hungary and Russia were condemned, but what about the violence of the revolutionaries themselves? Certain delegates felt that the use of force in the cause of social justice could not be opposed. And yet, could an organization that counseled against violence in international conflicts do otherwise in situations of internal strife? By only one vote, the congress resolved that the WILPF must maintain its faith in peaceful methods of effecting change, believing that it was "their special part in this revolutionary age to counsel against violence from any side" (Bussey and Tims 1980, 39).

Helena Swanwick was one of the few women delegates at the League of Nations fifth assembly in 1924. She was a rapporteur on the refugee question. In her 1935 autobiography, *I Have Been Young*, she complains bitterly about the way women were treated at the League.

Women, outside the closed doors, have to guess, to infer, to put two and two together, to reconstruct imaginatively what men are told by obsequious secretaries and industrious officials, or hear in conference or through dispatches. Men have access to mines of information closed to us (415).

Swanwick was a pacifist with strong, yet realistic views. She approved of compromise, for, as she said, "if everyone insists on their own way, what is there to do but fight for it?" Referring to President Wilson and the Kellogg Pact, she wrote, "In Wilson's words, there is such a thing as being too proud to fight." She went on to say "I don't call myself a Christian, but certainly I believe that Jesus was too proud to fight" (451). Swanwick believed in thinking, not fighting.

In these interwar years there was another important group of political women in Great Britain who were concerned not so much with questions of pacifism and disarmament as with women's social and political equality. They were known as the Six Point Group, founded in 1921 by Viscountess Rhondda with six specific aims in mind: (1) satisfactory legislation on child assault; (2) satisfactory legislation for the widowed mother; (3)

satisfactory legislation for the unmarried mother and her child; (4) equal rights of guardianship for married parents; (5) equal pay for men and women teachers; and (6) equality of opportunity for men and women in the Civil Service. These points later evolved into six general points of equality for women: political, occupational, moral, social, legal, and economic. Throughout its existence the Six Point Group, chaired by Monica Whateley during the thirties, stressed its feminism and its belief in practical politics; moreover, it always emphasized its nonparty stance. Such women as Elizabeth Robins, Winifred Holtby, Dorothy Evans, Sybil Morrison, Dora Russell, Monica Whateley, and for many years Hazel Hunkins-Halliman played active roles in the group's organization.

The Six Point Group worked with other women's groups and in particular with the Women's Freedom League, but they were not specifically antiwar. For example, although they supported the British Committee Against War and Fascism, they were rather put out when they were officially represented on the British section of the Women's World Committee Against War and Fascism in a demonstration in Trafalgar Square in September 1935. In the Hon. Secretary's report just after the demonstration, Miss Whateley made it clear that "We were co-operating only from the anti-fascist side as our members were divided on the question of the best peace policy, and we could not, therefore, officially have any views on the matter" (Fawcett Library Archives). When, on 23 June 1936 the Six Point Group was told that the British Committee Against War and Fascism was in financial difficulties and it was doubtful if they would be able to continue to publish their Bulletin, Whateley said she was opposed to any grant being given to the organization until she was convinced that they were pressing the antifascist side of their work with the same enthusiasm with which they were doing peace propaganda. Although the Six Point Group adequately comprehended the military threat that fascism signified, they did not fully perceive the menace fascism represented to women's rights, even though by this time the women's movement in Germany, which had been built up over sixty years, had been totally destroyed by the Nazis. In other words, the Six Point Group was antifascist but not because of the suppression of women's rights, of which they were largely though not entirely unaware.

Yet another important group of women who worked to inform the newly enfranchised British woman of her political rights and potential political power were the writers and editors of the women's magazines and the *Woman's Newspaper*. In the 1930s in Britain there was a fortnightly magazine, *Woman Today*, whose editorial emphasis was upon peace: "We struggle for peace and freedom, our rights and the protection of mother and child" (*Woman Today*, October 1937, in British Library Holdings, Colindale). The magazine was published by the British section of the Women's World Committee Against War and Fascism. An editorial in 1937 sounds a depressingly familiar complaint: "more and more is being spent for war every year, and when we get the more recent figures we shall probably find that the social services are being starved even more to pay for war services" (ibid.). This same magazine reported that the Women's Commission at the World Peace Congress in Brussels, 3 September 1938, declared, "If women do not struggle with all their strength against the coming of these horrors, let the blood of their sons be on their heads." The speaker was Romain Rolland (ibid.).

Helena Swanwick had once exclaimed to Catherine Marshall, "I want a good progressive daily paper so dreadfully! But I suppose a weekly is all we could ever dream of" (Wiltsher 1985, 74). Mrs. Swanwick's dream came true eventually, for in London between 1938 and 1939 the first independent woman's newspaper was published, controlled, and supported entirely by women—if only briefly. It began as a weekly, *Woman's National Newspaper;* became a daily, *Woman's Daily;* and then went back to its weekly format as *Woman's Newspaper*. The policy of the editor, Jean Stafford, was to inform women in England about the possibilities of keeping the peace, and there were editorial headings such as: "Let us Think Peace," "War is Not Inevitable," and "We Must Act for Peace" (British Library, Colindale). The newspaper became the official voice of the Women's League of Unity, an organization of peace-loving women, the majority of whom were not absolute pacifists. Once war was declared on 3 September 1939, they worked in any way they could to end it, as munition workers, service women, doctors, and nurses.

British Women's Magazines and International Women

British women's magazines and newspapers at this time covered the war in Spain and ever increasing Nazi threat in Germany itself, educating women in Britain about the plight of women in these countries as well as in Austria and Italy. Although in Spain in the thirties there was no organized women's movement, women workers did belong to trade unions. In 1936 some of these women became the *milicianas,* shouldering their rifles alongside the men in the defense of the government they had elected. A December 1936 issue of *Woman Today* carries a story illustrating the effect of these brave women on the men they fought next to, both equally untrained for war. The men could not bear to see the women injured and dying; the sight filled them with horror and a furious rage so that they lost all control apparently and went wildly at the enemy, calling them butchers and fascists and getting needlessly killed themselves (British Library, Colindale). Because of this Spanish chivalry the *milicianas* had to be gradually withdrawn.

The Spanish civil war was not only a crucial confrontation between fascism and democracy, but a conflict between a political system that totally degraded women, treating them as mere breeders, and a political system under which women were slowly gaining their political, economic, and personal rights. The Peace and Disarmament Committee of the Women's International Organization in Geneva published a strong condemnation of the situation in Spain at this time. One branch of this group, The League of Mothers and Educators for Peace, spoke in the following terms: "We have protested against the scandalous inaction of the so-called Committee of Non-Intervention in the Spanish conflict. We have joined our efforts and our protestations to everything which has been done to stop the bombardment of open towns and of civilian populations" (Press Release No. 220, June 1938, Peace and Disarmament Committee of the Women's International Organization). These sections cooperated fully in the relief work for Spanish refugees and collaborated with the Committee for Peace in Spain, which asked for an armistice and for consultation with the people of Spain so that they could decide their own future themselves.

In this twenty-year period between the two world wars, fascism was also plaguing other countries, Italy in particular. In Italy at this time Mussolini believed that war was as necessary to men as motherhood to women. Apparently many Italian women were not dismayed by this kind of thinking. Women's lives in Italy in the 1930s progressed mostly along feminine lines. These women seemed non-political; they did not seem to want a voice in the government. They were apparently content to let the men make the laws and were resigned to the fact that, economically, they could expect few privileges. The organization of the *Fasci Femminili* founded in the early years of Italian fascism, administered relief funds, secured hospital admissions, and organized soup kitchens, maternity and child welfare centers. Women were in some of the workers' trades unions at this time, but Italian women were not enfranchised until 1945.

In America there had been a National Committee on the Cause and Cure of War since 1924; it consisted of eleven nationwide women's organizations, such as the American Association of University Women, the National Committee of Jewish Women, and the Woman's Christian Temperance Union. These women struggled to make their country more aware of the need for international cooperation and peace. In 1937 they urged upon their senators and congressmen a foreign policy of active participation in the creation of world peace by economic cooperation and a modification of the neutrality isolationist policy, which treated aggressors and their victims alike. In 1939 the women openly advocated the expansion of relations between the U. S. and the League of Nations. These organizations worked in cooperation with the Peace and Disarmament Committee of the Women's International Organizations and the Peace Committee of the International Council of Women. This latter group of women, like other similar groups, such as WILPF, were committed to helping women as citizens to understand the nature of the problems of peace and war. With this goal in mind the Peace and Disarmament Committee organized special study conferences, mostly in Europe. The last of these was held in Zurich in February 1937. The general title of the sessions was "A Practical Peace Policy," which was discussed at a series of roundtable conferences covering such questions as:

> Can Treaties be regarded as sacred unless there is effective machinery available for peaceful change? How can the profits of the manufacture of and traffic in arms be eliminated? How can we organise collective security and mutual assistance? Should we favour the resummoning of the Disarmament Conference to attempt the achievement of a limited Convention? How can we establish within the framework of the League of Nations effective machinery for remedying international conditions which might lead to war? (Fawcett Library Archives)

Commendable, but very, very large questions.

Political Women in Germany, 1919–1933

Striking similarities as well as differences existed among the political, social, and domestic conditions of women in Britain and Germany between the two world wars.

The women's movement in Germany had begun in the 1860s, but, as in Britain, it was the 1914 war that gave women the chance to prove themselves through increased opportunities in industry, welfare work, nursing, medicine, and education. Women were not conscripted into industry, as were all civilian men under the Hindenburg Programme of 1916, but they were strongly encouraged to volunteer, and working-class women did so in great numbers. Their reward was a moderate narrowing of wage differentials, so that by the end of the war their pay rose to about half of men's wage rates. In 1914, Gertrud Bäumer, leader of the middle-class conservative League of German Women's Associations, founded the *Bund Deutscher Frauenvereine* (BDF), or the National Women's Service, to mobilize volunteers for welfare work and for making clothing for the armed forces. Large numbers of middle-class women also volunteered for the Red Cross.[7]

During the war, as we have seen, the Women's Suffrage League, led by the left-wing pacifists Lida Gustava Heymann and Anita Augspurg, had continuously campaigned for peace and female suffrage until the authorities clamped down on them in May 1916. But their numbers were small, just like the pacifist women's groups in Britain, compared with the massive middle-class BDF. From the beginning of the war until 1917 the BDF had a greater influence, actually campaigning against emancipation, emphasizing instead nationalism, social welfare, and education. Recall that Emmeline Pankhurst as leader of the powerful Women's Social and Political Union (WSPU) in Britain had also been prepared to sacrifice the women's vote. Like Mrs. Fawcett's National Union of Women's Suffrage Societies (NUWSS), the BDF put nationalism and patriotism before women's political rights, throwing all their energy into the war effort. And, like Mrs. Fawcett and Emmeline Pankhurst, Gertrud Bäumer thought that ensuring women's war efforts was the best way to achieve the right climate of opinion to obtain female suffrage after the war. In Britain, however, suffragists kept an eye on the emancipation issue, even when they were engaged in war work, and when the time came (summer 1916), they sent depositions to Westminster to ensure that women's suffrage should be part of a new franchise bill if the Asquith government fell. Similarly, a year later in Germany, the BDF began to campaign heavily for women's emancipation, which was granted on 12 November 1918.

Happily, the revolutionary overthrow of the imperial regime in Germany in November 1918 and the signing of the armistice in

1919 forcibly removed an important obstacle to women's advancement and their enfranchisement in particular: the Kaiser. The caretaker Socialist government was quick to extend the suffrage to women, and the election of forty-one women deputies— almost ten percent of the membership of the Reichstag—in 1919 seemed to bode well (Stephenson 1975, 15). Women would now be able to take their rightful place in the reconstruction of a revolutionary new Germany following defeat and exhaustion in the war.

Cross-cultural comparisons are always problematic because what is being compared may not be exactly the same. Apparently the same phenomena in two or more cultures may in fact have little in common. Thus to look, however briefly, at the women in Germany who were the first elected representatives after emancipation, and compare them with their counterparts in Britain may suggest debatable comparisons. Nevertheless, there is no question that only one woman was elected to the first Parliament in Britain on 28 December 1918, whereas in the caretaker Socialist government in Germany in January 1919 forty-one women members were elected to the Reichstag. There are several possible explanations here. First, and most important, is that gaining the vote for women on 12 November 1918, was partly the result of the social revolution that was sweeping Germany. The political situation was increasingly desperate from 5 November on when sailors revolted at Kiel and workers' and soldiers' councils were being set up all over the country to overthrow the government. In the confusion and chaos that followed these events, the demand for female suffrage, most forcibly voiced by the *Sozialdemokratische Partei Deutschlands* (SPD) won the day. Some commentators therefore argue that it was not the pacifist or nationalist feminists that won German women the vote but the prevailing revolutionary conditions in Germany in early November 1918 (Evans 1976, 266–67). In any case, it was a dearly won vote. On the other hand, Kirkpartrick believes that the women's "heroic war effort" helped them to be enfranchised by the Weimar constitution (1938, 55–56).

Another important difference between the political situation in Britain and Germany was that this first government in Germany after World War I was predominantly a socialist revolutionary one, supported by both women and men, whereas in Britain the government elected on 28 December 1918 was a coalition government mainly supported by the male population.

In Germany at this time women were also more aware of the

workplace as a political space, thanks to such pioneering trade unionists as Liselotte Hermann of Bavaria, the Marxist theoretician Rosa Luxemburg,[8] and her friends Clara Zetkin and Karl Leibknecht. Evidently those British working women who went on working in the 1920s and 1930s (in spite of the Labour Party's continued insistence on women remaining at home) were not as well organized or politically supported in the workplace as their German counterparts.

In the early years of postwar Germany women and some men were apparently more politically aware of the importance of getting women elected to government positions than they were in Britain. In the 1920s in Germany the socialist analysis of women's oppression continued to shape the Social Democratic women and their emphasis upon economic inequality.

Here it is important to remember that, as a legacy of World War I, the majority of German feminists were unmarried. Kirkpatrick's figures show that there were almost two million "extra" women in postwar Germany (1938, 40–51). Consequently they had an urgent need to fight for women's rights in the workplace (and thus the accusation could later be leveled at them that they did not represent the ordinary German mother and wife). In his seminal book, *Nazi Germany: Its Women and Family Life*, (Kirkpatrick) writes that "No discussion of German women can ignore that vast unknown army whose sacrifice of marital happiness was one of the less obvious war losses." He goes on to say that at this time German women twenty-four or older outnumbered the actual potential husbands. Those men who might have provided these women with happy marriages were buried under the wooden crosses of Ypres, Krakow, and Verdun. "In 1933, not counting the Saarland, there were still 1,834,397 extra women" (127). These tragic circumstances also of course afflicted British women. For the enormous numbers of bereaved women in England it also became a necessity to work for their living whether they wanted to or not. The need to work was a new phenomenon of historical significance.

The first woman to deliver a speech as a national representative in the Reichstag on 11 February 1919 was justifiably triumphant:

> I should like to say now that the "woman question" in Germany no longer exists in the old sense of the term; it has been solved. It will no longer be necessary for us to campaign for our rights with meetings, resolutions and petitions. Political conflict, which will always exist,

will from now on take place in another form. We women now have the opportunity to allow our influence to be exerted within the context of party groupings on the basis of ideology. (Quoted in Stephenson 1975, 16)

But the hope implicit in these sentiments of Marie Juchaczo took only a decade to prove illusory, and the claims premature.[9] By 1930 the radical feminists in Germany were convinced that progress towards equality for women had been frustrated throughout the 1920s because of the continuing majority of men in every parliamentary party (Stephenson 1975, 17). This situation paralleled that in Britain for all of the interwar years. Throughout the 1920s in Germany the Social Democrat women continued to believe that August Bebel's 1904 book, *Woman Under Socialism*, was the definitive work on the woman question. That these women never abandoned socialist ideas or recognized the limitations of the socialist interpretation of women's plight was not their chief cause of failure; rather it was probably because they did not go beyond the socialist analysis of women's position. By the 1930s, although socialist theory in general recognized that the oppression of women preceded capitalism, it did not draw the logical conclusion that the oppression of women in patriarchal and capitalist societies was economic *and* psychosexual.

International socialism as a movement has always been pledged to the equality of women, especially in economic terms. But a conflict of interest may be recognized between the socialist women in Germany and Britain and the massive middle-class groups in both countries who had worked so ardently for the suffrage movement. This latter group did not necessarily believe that once women were not oppressed in the workplace they would attain political and sexual equality with men. On the other hand, the socialist analysis of society in Britain and Germany was largely a class analysis which viewed women's oppression as being due entirely to the capitalist system; what this analysis failed to take into account was the various other kinds of oppression under which women suffered, such as property rights, divorce, education, and parental rights. Women's rights over their sexuality are important—what is most one's own should not be taken away from one—but the formulation of this belief was not as important or central to women's socialist thought as perhaps it should have been, and possibly because of this failure in emphasis, women did not receive the electoral support they might otherwise have gotten in Germany or in Britain. In other words, feminism and socialism are not necessarily two sides of the same coin; some feminists do not want to be socialists, and some socialists do not want to be feminists. They might accomplish more if they joined forces.

Socialist theory is useful for understanding the particular nature of the oppression of women under capitalism; however, it is not very useful for understanding their oppression as women. A good case can be made for the idea that women are oppressed because they are women, and not for some other reason.[10]

Perhaps a reconceptualization might eventually have evolved out of the Social Democratic women's movement in Germany if the entire women's movement had not been destroyed by the advent of fascism (Pore 1981, 51; Rupp 1978, 13–15; Stephenson 1975, 16). Even before all the parties were dissolved in Germany in 1933 and the Nazis were in unchallenged control of the state, it was clear that no branch of the women's movement was to be allowed to remain in existence. Women's political support was expected to be verbal only, not active. All women, including Nazi women, were forbidden from holding seats in the Reichstag or any high-powered political office.

German Peace Women Between the Wars

The German branch of WILPF was very active in the 1920s and early 1930s. Indeed, two of the founding members of The Hague Congress of 1915 out of which WILPF was formed were the eminent German women Dr. Anita Augspurg, the first woman judge in Germany, and the pioneer feminist and trade union organizer from Bavaria, Lida Gustava Heymann. The German WILPF certainly promoted the ideal of internationalism, so important a belief to all members of the organization, and in January 1929 they hosted a full meeting of the league in Frankfurt. In 1932 another conference of all international women's pacifist organizations was held in Munich under the chairmanship of the local WILPF leader, Constanze Hallgarten. This meeting was reported by the Nazis under the title "Pacifist Scandal in Munich."

The decision of International WILPF to advocate peaceful change was of great importance in the league's national sections, above all in Germany where pacifists had offered heroic examples of pioneering, nonviolent action. As Bussey and Tims point out, the successful general strike against the Kapp putsch in

Berlin in 1920 is perhaps the most celebrated of these actions (39). But it was not an isolated case. In Hamburg, Munich, Jena, and other cities, "white" Prussian troops attacked the democratic Weimar Republic, with counterattacks from the extreme left. In all these disturbances, German women members of WILPF took an active and often dangerous reconciling role. In Munich Gertrude Baer led a small mission to negotiate between the "white" and "red" forces encamped outside the city, obtaining the promise from both sides that neither would shoot first. Again in Jena, WILPF members pleaded successfully with Zeiss workers to stay off the street and close down the factories so that Prussian troops had no pretext to fire (Bussey & Tims 39). This same Gertrude Baer was the German delegate to the League of Nations' committee on youth affairs, as well as a representative at the League's International Disarmament discussions. Because of her "outspokenly pacifist and feminist outlook" she was dismissed from public service by the Nazis in 1933 and from 1935 to 1937 was denied the right to publish her writings. She escaped from Germany in 1938, and during the Second World War she managed the New York office of WILPF.

The End of the Women's Movement in Germany

Hitler's opposition to the participation of women in politics and his low opinion of women's abilities are well known; women were, for Hitler, mere breeders of future armies. In a speech in April 1932 he made his famous promise: "What has the Revolution of 1918 actually done for women? All it has done is to turn fifty thousand of them into blue stockings and party officials. Under the Third Reich they might as well whistle for such things. Every women will get a husband for herself."[11] Aside from anything else, this promise cruelly ignored the fact that there were not in any case enough husbands, as Kirkpatrick's figures clearly show. On the other hand, young couples were putting off marrying because of the bleak economic situation.

Hitler's main idea for women was to keep them in the home where their duty was to bear children to make the future armies of the Vaterland. Nazi leaders were aware that their emphasis upon the exclusive childbearing role assigned to women was by some critics considered demeaning. In his 1935 party day speech to the National Socialist *Frauenschaft* (founded in 1931), the childless Hitler answered these critics by asserting that it was in no way degrading to a woman to be a mother; quite the contrary, it was her greatest honor and noblest achievement to provide sons and daughters for the Vaterland and the Fuehrer.

It is but a short step from this ideal to that of German woman as soldier's mother or wife. In other words, the Nazis required women to sacrifice their political rights for their duties as mothers and wives. The Labour Party in England had tended to pressure women in the same way although not for the same reasons.[12] To this end the Nazis instituted marriage loans, encouraging those would could not afford to marry to do so. The doctrine that every good German woman should have five children to ensure the necessary number "for the nation" completely undid the work of the Social Democratic women who, in the 1920s, had taken the lead in campaigning for progressive legislation in abortion, marriage, and divorce reform.[13]

Indeed, every point on which the separate women's groups had agreed in the 1920s was out of the question for the NSDAP: internationalism, feminism, pacifism, and individualism were totally unacceptable ideas, to be ruthlessly eliminated. Indeed, all left-wing thought was anathema to the Nazis, who were committed to destroying it. On the other hand, the National Socialist movement in Germany appealed to a wide range of other special interest groups and to all social classes. Rempel writes that "Its very diversity was a source of strength in a period of political disillusionment and economic uncertainty" (1989, 256).

By the 1930s, radical feminists in Germany had to face the devastating threat of Hitler's fascism. Yet it is clear from Koonz's important book, *Mothers in the Fatherland*, that a great many women were united in support of the Nazi party despite the party ban on all non-Nazi groups in 1933. Koonz writes that women "nearly as strongly as men supported the Nazi party during its rise in 1930 and 1932" (1987, 45). Her book deals mostly with the early years of the Nazi regime and is based upon a very forceful and painful assumption: "Far from being innocent, women made possible a murderous state" and, furthermore, they did so "in the name of concerns they defined as motherly" (45). Yet they seemed unaware of or indifferent to the fact that this collaboration with the Nazi state exploited them by denying them access to political status, depriving them of birth control, underpaying them, and indoctrinating their children and recruiting their menfolk to the battle-fronts of North Africa, Russia, and Europe. The separation of masculine and feminine worlds, which followed logically and psychologically from the Nazi leaders' misogyny, placed woman below the dominant man in every respect.

Paradoxically, Koonz's thesis is that the Nazi regime rested on a feminine system of support, and her investigation of the top Nazi woman, Gertrud Scholtz-Klink provides ample evidence to support her argument: *Reichsfrauenführerin* (Women's Leader of the Reich) Scholtz-Klink "saw herself as the chief of a lobby for women's concerns and as the leader of women missionaries who would bring Nazi doctrine 'home' to every family in the Reich. Far from remaining untouched by Nazi evil, women operated at its very center" (Koonz 1987, 6).[14]

As background to the Nazi ideology Koonz describes the conflicts over the "woman question" in the Weimar era and the emergence, especially in Berlin, of the intellectually and sexually assertive "new woman" who frightened men. Koonz also describes the reaction against various women's groups advocating militant feminism as opposed to a more gentle womanly ideal (12). The Nazis of course manipulated both sides of this conflict. It was a political tragedy that the various women's groups—radical, conservative, Catholic, and Protestant—did not unite against a party that was inimical to them all, including their children, especially their teenage daughters and sons who were forced into the Hitler Jugend (HJ), or Hitler Youth, and ruthlessly and often brutally politically conditioned.

Within the context of women's experience in Nazi Germany in the period between the two world wars, it is of the utmost importance to consider the fate of the children. The intense social pressure parents were under to have their children sign up as members of the HJ cannot be ignored. Neither can the degraded, tragic lives of these children ever be adequately compensated for, even if their prime architect, Baldur von Schirach, was given a heavy sentence at Nuremberg.

"The Nazi party was a party of the young" and Hitler betrayed all their young idealism and loyalty, according to Rempel (1989, 256). He continues:

The Nazi movement could not have expanded and kept its youthful character without SS terrorism and without the HJ becoming an important element in the movement before the assumption of power. As a mass organization, incorporating nearly the entire younger generation in the twelve years that followed, the HJ sustained the movement's vitality. (257)

But what did the mothers think of their children being mobilized in this fashion? How did they feel about the state condition-
ing their daughters and sons to serve it alone, teaching them to
spy on their parents, and indoctrinating them with the idea that
ideological war must end in victory or annihilation? This last
pernicious idea encouraged the fatalistic sacrifice of those
seventeen- and eighteen-year-olds who fought against the Allies
in France and Belgium at the very end of the war. For example,
at the incredibly brutal battle of Caen in northern France in 1944
there were ten thousand casualties among the soldiers known as
the "Young Grenadiers," all of whom had been recruited from
the HJ.

But there was even worse in store for these young men than
that devastating battle with the Americans and Canadians. Just
before their SS-Panzer regiment reached the next line of attack,
they met a group of ferocious Belgian guerrillas. The grim story
of this encounter is told by Butler in *Hitler's Young Tigers:*

> The partisans had mined the roads; young men screamed as a series
> of explosions sliced off their legs. The partisans were not soldiers
> and had none of the soldier's code of honour when it came to
> fighting. They shot their opponents in the back or leapt on them and
> slit their throats. (1986, 129)

These were the young men who had so optimistically given their
loyalty and energy to Hitler and his menacing demands: "I want a
youth, a cruel, unflinching youth, as hard as steel—Krupp steel."

Under von Schirach the HJ was entirely male. Once Artur Axmann took it over in the late 1930s girls were recruited into the
Bund Deutscher Mädchen (BDM) for one year to help on farms.
But besides helping with the harvest, many of these young
women were getting pregnant, much to their parents' dismay.
Morality was not of real concern to the leaders of these male
and female youth organizations, for the begetting of pure Aryan
children was highly desirable.

In order to justify and even encourage such developments, in
September 1940 an SS decree was issued urging "German
women of good blood" to become mothers by soldiers fighting
at the front (Butler 1986, 84). This program was known as *Lebensborn,* (a breeding establishment), whereby girls went to special
camps to meet young soldiers and beget children. The girls had
to be medically examined and their ancestry investigated before

their "patriotic honeymoon" could begin. Moreover, these mothers could make no claims upon any child they might have.[15] Parents who objected to this treatment of their daughters were in danger of displeasing the powerful Himmler. It was no doubt better to remain quietly waiting for the return of their daughters than to be in prison when they arrived home again. It is small wonder that the fate of the young men and women of the HJ has been referred to as the rape of a generation, a modern massacre of the innocents.

Rempel's analysis of "Hitler's children" concludes by saying that these doomed young people were betrayed, deserted, and sacrificed by a party and a regime that had used them to attain power. Far from being a streamlined version of the Boy Scouts and Girl Scouts, "The experience of this generation, instead of evoking a picture of sardonic relief from the sombre realities of Himmler's black-coated engineers of terror and death, reveals a new dimension of the Third Reich" (1989, 263).

For the Nazis, a "genuine" woman was expected to pay homage to the "masculine principle"; only then would she become "a real woman." Hitler's three Ks,—"Kirche, Kinder, and Küche" (church, children, and kitchen)—were of great appeal to many middle-class traditional women; these values seemed appropriate and virtuous, since they supported a way of life many women wanted. Ironically, this group thought that women who wanted to work outside the home were indecent. Koonz documents the way in which the Nazis infiltrated secular, Catholic, and Protestant women's groups, despite the fact that many of these groups were clearly embittered by the coarseness of Nazi male domination and the way the regime humiliated women, as well as by repeated betrayals of women leaders in not granting them political power.

Yet there were significant female contributions to Nazi ideology: The self-congratulatory Nazi woman, Scholtz-Klink said in an interview: "Our job (and we do it well) is to infuse the daily life of all German women with Nazi ideals." According to Koonz, Scholtz-Klink's social workers, teachers, and nurses turned over the names of the mentally retarded, schizophrenics, alcoholics, and misfits to Nazi sterilization agencies. Kirkpatrick (1938) makes the point that Scholtz-Klink had a vast and intricate organization of women under her control and that she stressed the advantage of her organization, the *Frauenwerk*, a single federal body, in contrast to earlier women's groups because it included all social classes within its vast membership. In her own words:

There is hardly a state in which the total work of women is so
brought together under one hand as in Germany. The National
Woman's Leadership has been active in advising and in shaping
every law that has importance for women. (72)

Undoubtedly, Gertrud Scholtz-Klink, herself the mother of six
children, two of whom had died in infancy, was a woman of
fanatical energy whose unscrupulousness and total submission
to Nazi ideology had brought her the leadership of all the Nazi
women's groups. She was ultimately responsible for the dissolu-
tion of the powerful and massive BDF whose revered leader, Gertrud Bäumer, was forced to dissolve its constitution in May 1933.

Most commentators on Nazi ideology agree that the Nazis' argument for "separate spheres," for sending men off to war to
protect mothers and children and the family home, sanctioned
the violence of war.[16] On the other hand, Leila Rupp in *Mobilizing Women for War* distinguishes between Nazi ideology and
Nazi propaganda. She argues that while the Nazi ideology insisted woman's place was in the home, the propaganda stressed
that "woman's place was in the war" (1978, 136). However, at the
beginning of the war it seems the propaganda effort was sometimes less successful than the ideological one. At the beginning,
apparently, not all German women wanted their men to leave
them and go to war. In August 1939 the British newspaper
Woman Today quoted an antifascist German bulletin: "At the
departure of newly mobilised troops from Berlin railway sta-
tions, the women refused to let their men get into the trains.
Screaming and protesting, the women and children clung to the
men" (British Library, Colindale). This too, of course, can be
construed as propaganda.

Both Rupp and Koonz agree that the Nazi woman "in all her
roles created the spirit out of which the strength of the army
grew" (Rupp 1978, 135). That is to say, although the woman's
primary job was to take care of her family, she was also expected
to make munitions for her sons at war and contribute in as many
ways as possible to the war effort. Women might engage in any
number of activities, but in the public image, all these became
extensions of their central function as mothers. As air-raid wardens women fulfilled their most important duty, the protection
of their families. As workers in munitions factories, women cared
for their sons by making the ammunition they needed at the
front. Rupp quotes one woman working in a munitions factory
while her son was at the front. She summed up her function as

follows: "Earlier I buttered bread for him, now I paint grenades and think, this is for him" (1978, 122).

Furthermore, during the Allied bombing of German cities, particularly in the summer and autumn of 1943, these mothers and wives were exhorted to match their courage to endure and sacrifice with that which their menfolk showed in battle. This same encouragement to share with the men at the front the fearsome destructiveness and horrifying injuries of war, and to be brave and endure the terrors of aerial bombardment, was experienced by British women, too, during the blitz of their cities. In both countries the women earned tremendous admiration for their courage in these horrendous conditions. In Nazi Germany this courage gained the women the title of "soldiers of the homeland."

Not all women fell under Hitler's evil spell, but those who actively resisted his policies did so at great personal risk. Some of these women, like Gertrude Baer of German WILPF, were hounded out of the country and their writings were destroyed. Of those few brave hundreds who were heroically active in working against Hitler and the Nazi regime from 1933 onward, many were imprisoned and some died in prison. Right at the beginning of the Hitler era a deputation of British women went to Germany to visit some of these courageously defiant women in Nazi prisons. They did not succeed in their mission; Hitler did not want the world to hear stories of the fearless women who opposed him. That the German women's opposition just before the outbreak of World War II, though small in number, was taken seriously, is evident by the appalling fact that on 21 June 1938 on the charge of treason, Hitler had beheaded with an axe the daring antifascist woman who was such an inspiration to other German women, Liselotte ("Lilo") Hermann. The British newspaper, Woman Today (June 1938) carried the story of this brave woman and others like her in their fight against fascism.[17]

A reporter gives an Austrian woman's account in November 1938 describing the effect of Nazism in Vienna after the Germans had taken over on 11 March that year:

". . . thousands of women's voices swelled the cry of Hail Victory!" The Fascist movement had many women supporters in student circles, who visualised their ideal in a Nazi state, and easily won members among the Post Office employees and civil servants, whom they had persuaded that Hitler would bring paradise on earth to his followers. But shortly afterwards the leaders made announcements on the radio, and the women heard something quite different. Restrain yourselves, they heard. Do without things and work hard. You must bear children for the Nazi regime, and these are only entrusted to you to look after for a short time, since they belong to the Nazi Party! As mothers they lost their influence over their children, who until late at night were forced to take part in so-called "Triumphal Processions." Their sons were forced into the army and their daughters into the labour camps. A girl of 17 wrote to her mother that she was pregnant. But as a consolation she wrote: "Thirty-five other girls here are in the same condition." (*Woman Today*, November 1938)

On 29 September 1939, on its "Women in War" page, the *London Evening News* quoted another Viennese woman who had broadcast an appeal to the women of Germany to "help to end the cruel and unnecessary war by co-operating in overthrowing the criminal and mad regime of the Nazis." The woman's broadcast over "Freedom" Radio Station continued:

Where is our freedom now and where our dignity and our happiness? All raped by a lunatic. This happened 18 months ago, but have you, you German women, become happier because Hitler has robbed our country? . . . No. The only consequence is that your husbands and sons are now dying. (*International Women's News*, 35, 2, [December 1940])

If only those women who actively resisted Hitler and those other international women who were speaking out against fascism and its immense threat to women and men, as well as to a peaceful Europe, had spoken with one voice and presented a united front, perhaps they would have been able to politicize women's international awareness of their role as an emancipated force for peace and freedom. What was needed was a united international women's party that could speak with one voice. But it would have been an enormously complex task. Evidently the most sinister aspect of the Nazi threat for German women was it attractiveness, as well as their unwillingness to actually analyze its significance in their lives.

In fact women's enfranchisement in Germany up until Hitler's takeover in 1933 meant only that they were now physically represented, albeit in greater numbers than in Britain; however, even these politically aware women remained largely powerless in the forming of government policies, as were the women parliamentarians of Great Britain.

The Imminence of War and Women's Continuing Peace Efforts in Britain

By 1937 the menace of war was quite clear; the League of Nations was in disarray, and fascism was disastrous for peace. The work of peacemakers everywhere became enormously difficult; however, rather than slowing these people down, the threatening situation intensified their efforts to keep the peace. The Committee of Peace and Disarmament of the Women's International Organizations resisted in their publications the idea, more and more accepted, of war, immediate and inevitable; the folly of super armaments, which ruin all budgets; and the abandonment of the League of Nations and its methods.

The rise of fascism in Germany, Italy, and Spain made pacifism and disarmament seem perhaps foolhardy, even treacherous. Women's efforts to help limit international aggression and to educate women politically for peace proved once more to be an unequal task. New means had to be imagined for reconciling the demands of both peace and justice.

In Britain the membership of WILPF was mostly middle class, but the Women's League of Unity, formed in September 1938, did provide an organized leadership for working women whose manifest wish was for peace. A statement put out by the league declared: "Nobody doubts the devotion of women as a whole to the cause of peace and civilized progress. But individual woman feels she can do little to change the conditions that lead to war. UNITED WE CAN STOP WAR" (British Library, Colindale). This was an important manifesto, although it went unheeded, because only through joint action of women of all classes and parties can the collective power of women be organized to speak with one voice for peace.

Although the organization of the Women's League of Unity and the *Woman's Newspaper* (1938–39) were separate, there were close ties between them; indeed, the newspaper actively encouraged women to join the league by printing subscription forms within the format of the newspaper. In the 6 September 1939 issue, Jean Stafford, editor-in-chief of the *Woman's Newspaper*, published two forceful messages she had sent in August on behalf of British women. One was to Mrs. Roosevelt in Washington and the other to the British prime minister, Neville Chamberlain. The desperate last-minute cable Jean Stafford sent to Mrs. Roosevelt on 24 August 1939 reads (in part):

World civilization threatened. . . . Woman's Newspaper, Fleet Street, London, England, urges Mrs. Roosevelt to support British women's appeal to avert catastrophe of untold misery for innocent women and children from bombs and bacteria. If the United States will join peace front such action will save civilization. In the name of women and children who may have to make the supreme sacrifice will you act now? (British Library, Colindale)

I have not been able to find a reply to this cable. To Chamberlain the editor's letter, dated August 29, 1939, read in part:

As Editor of Woman's Newspaper, I write in the name of the women of Great Britain. . . It may seem presumptuous to make suggestions at this time, but those that follow are sent with an earnest desire to help.
I wish to submit the following proposals:
1. That an immediate request be made to Germany, Poland, France and Russia, Italy and all countries whose troops are massed on the many frontiers, to agree to withdraw their forces for at least five miles from each frontier with the undertaking that they should remain withdrawn for one month.
2. That an immediate conference of the Great Powers of the world be called to meet in conference during that month on neutral soil to review and discuss the whole of the problems that are keeping humanity in a state of suspense and turmoil, and that an attempt be made to settle them by peaceful negotiation.
3. I suggest that a Neutral Chairman chosen from one of the smaller independent neutral states be asked to preside over this gathering which would be literally an International Parliament which would lead to decisions worthy of the civilized world. (ibid.)

This letter was anything but "presumptuous" but it was far, far too late. Although there were active branches of the WILPF in America, half the members resigned at the outbreak of war in 1939. Most probably those who left had never been conscientious pacifists.[18] Neither were the British women who joined the Woman's League for Unity; they were women who wanted peace and were prepared to work for it during peacetime, but once war came then they set about working to win it in every way possible: as members of the armed services, land-army workers, air-raid wardens, ambulance drivers, and munition workers. The cause of peace is a very difficult one to espouse during wartime, especially when the war being waged is against such a monstrous evil as Nazi Germany. In the next chapter on World War II I shall explore the vicissitudes of pacifism when its expounders were faced with the monstrous evil of the Nazi state.

When we think about the welfare of international women during the period between the wars, it is sobering to realize how much woman's self-image was vitally shaped by three very powerful men who did not have women's interests at heart: Stalin, Mussolini, and Hitler. Stalin attacked the "bourgeois ideal" of family life, dethroned woman from the home, and proclaimed her a comrade of man, entitled to share both his burden and his rewards. Mussolini saw woman as the mother of fighting men and women saw themselves as playing a vital if not glorious part in their country's history. Hitler defined woman's duties as those of the nursery and kitchen. Fascism stressed woman's importance to the state so long as she was prepared to keep within her own sphere. Communism told woman that her role as woman was infinitely less than her role as a worker, that the hand that rocks the cradle is equally capable of firing a machine-gun or riveting a battleship. These two opposing ideological viewpoints have only one thing in common: both demand the sacrifice of the individual woman to the welfare of the state. In fascism as in the communism of this period in history, an entire generation of women, with notable exceptions, grew up molded from childhood to ideals so closely identified with the state as master that their way became the accepted model for the majority of women in Russia, Italy and Germany, and in Spain too after the civil war (1936–39). That this ideological pattern denied these women any individual political freedom or status was a lesson their more democratically aware sisters both in their own countries and abroad had to teach them.

Educating women for democracy was a long-term aim of many of the women's peace organizations in America, Europe, and Britain, such as WILPF and the Women's League for Unity; it was also the aim of pacifist women writers such as Vera Brittain, Helena Swanwick, and Virginia Woolf. However, if goals are to be realized there must be a method, a practical method for achieving them, and this these organizations failed to have. Perhaps the peace groups were too idealistic about the power they had for creating the necessary psychology for war resistance, although not all of these ideals were destroyed during the war, as we shall see in the next chapter. Or perhaps the problem was that the majority of women did not work hard enough for peace. Certainly these international groups were much too divided among themselves and each other. More prewar solidarity amongst women of the warring nations might perhaps have produced a more powerful will to peace—especially after women's emancipation in Britain and Germany, and before women were forbidden to be members of the Reichstag in 1933 and before the last general election before the war in Britain in 1935. It seems it was not possible for these groups to sink their differences of class, education, national, and political allegiances and so speak with one voice, act as one body. If the international collective power of women had been exercised, men and women might not, in that late, lovely summer of 1939, have had to burrow holes in the ground to save themselves and their children from the explosive nightmare of the air raids over British and German cities.

What women needed was to show the international significance of women's inferior political status and the way in which this status affected what women could achieve internationally in the vital cause of creating the will for a war-resisting psychology for everyone, so that as that psychology became strong, it could lead governments to pursue peace policies through negotiation and arbitration.

In Great Britain in 1939 women were not that much further on than on that summer night in August 1914 when women of Austria, Germany, Hungary, Belgium, France, America, and Britain itself, came out of the International Peace Conference in the Kingsway Hall, where they had passed a unanimous resolution against war, only to be told that the prime minister had declared war actually during their meeting. It was this shocking lack of a legislative voice that greatly advanced the cause of women's suffrage during that war. In the months, weeks, and days of crisis before the declaration of World War II there was no woman in the cabinet, although there were twelve women in Parliament at this time, including two vehement antiwar protesters, Ellen Wilkinson and Eleanor Rathbone. Once more women had to wait on the deliberations of cabinet councils where no woman's voice was heard. Once more British women had to put their entire trust in a political system whose ultimate decision-making power was in the hands of men only, just as it was in Germany. International solidarity should indeed have been the call.

4

Women's Experience of World War II: Britain and Germany

Women in Parliament

In the late summer of 1939, the hopes of an important woman writer *before* World War I had yet to be fulfilled. In her famous book on equal partnership in the house and in the workplace, *Woman and Labour* (1911), Olive Schreiner wrote:

> On that day, when the woman takes her place beside the man in the governance and arrangement of external affairs of her race will also be that day that heralds the death of war as a means of arranging human differences. (170)

On quite another day, that fateful 3 September 1939, no doubt many people thought it idle to speculate whether or not World War II could have been avoided had any of the twelve female Members of Parliament held cabinet positions in the government. In fact, there had been only one woman in the cabinet since 1919, Margaret Bondfield, who was Minister of Labour from 1929–1931. However, in the New Year's Honours List of 1945 both Florence Horsbrugh and Ellen Wilkinson, then junior ministers, were (at Churchill's suggestion) made Privy Councillors. (Members of an inner group of advisors to the Crown.) They were the first women to receive this honor since Margaret Bondfield. Both Ellen Wilkinson and Eleanor Rathbone were antiwar members of the House and had been actively involved in the debate on appeasement. By 1937 Wilkinson was calling for the formation of a popular front with the Communists, but this was rejected by the Labour Party. In 1938 Rathbone published her book, *War Can Be Averted,* in which she argued that war could be averted only if the League of Nations were prepared to stand up to aggression by using limited military force if necessary. The theme of her book was a development of ideas originating with the Duchess of Atholl. But although the number of women in Parliament during the war years was so small, they did manage to act as a feminist pressure group and, according to Brookes, almost as a women's party in ignoring party lines. "Few opportunities were lost by this very active group of women to uphold the rights and dignity of their sex" (1967, 139).

There may be some truth in the view that the Depression of the 1930s limited the feminist movement (Higonnet 1987, 43). But if instead of a minority, the majority of the women electorate between the two world wars had worked steadfastly for peace, by trying to influence political attitudes for example, there might have been much more of a dialogue. Once again women found themselves precipitated into a world war by a male dominated parliament. Once again political history was happening *to* women rather than being formed to some extent *by* women.

During the twenty years of their emancipation the majority of women had achieved some important rights, but although they were equal in voting rights, they were not equal in influencing those in power. Social justice and professional interests—rather than working to acquire political equality with men—had attracted women's services. No doubt women thought and hoped discrimination against them after World War I would disappear; it did not. Numerically, they were not that much better represented politically than during the First World War. What women had needed to do in the twenties and thirties was to solidify their political power so that they could vitally affect the policy of their country. Once more war had happened; human beings— British and German, women and men—had proved capable of making it happen because they had not sufficiently intelligently examined the forces ranged against peace.[1] The horror of war had once again materialized, and it had to be participated in and endured; or opposed.

The war had a profound impact on women's lives psychologically, socially, and economically, sowing the seeds of the future women's movement of the 1960s and 1970s and the eventual advance to almost full economic and social status with men. At the end of the war, an even greater destructive force was added to the immense horror, devastation, and loss it had caused: the atomic bomb. After this deadly weapon was unleashed upon Hiroshima and Nagasaki in August 1945, women and men all over the world grimly recognized the urgent need for a new analysis and clarification of the whole complex situation as a prerequisite for a constructive peace. With the founding of the United Nations in 1945 in San Francisco, international peaceworkers, both women and men, at last had a positive political aim: to save all humanity from total destruction. The reality of this terrifying possibility resulted in a greater than ever participation in the postwar peace movements. Ironic? Yes. Vital? As never before. The appalling fact of two world wars within a single generation—the second so much more violent in every way than the first, with its gas chambers for Jews, homosexuals, gypsies, communists; its mass "precision bombing"; its execution of innocent hostages; its Japanese suicide pilots; and its ghastly finale of nuclear radiation—conclusively proved just how militaristic and inhuman humanity had become.

Pacifist Women: "No More War"

Women did not enter the war without protest, but the "no more war" convictions of the 1920s had become more and more uncertain as the fascist threat against democracy increased in Germany, Italy, and Spain. In spite of the "terrible, inert mass of lethargic womanhood" (Berry and Bishop 1985, 217) and the many unavailing letters she wrote in the 1930s to the newspapers, accusing women in general of not caring enough about peace and not working hard enough to promote it, Vera Brittain said in 1934 in the magazine *Modern Woman:* "I believe the women of the world could stop war if they ceased to be completely absorbed in themselves and their homes and their children, and began to realize that their duty to mankind extends beyond their own little doorstep" (ibid., 218). But of course it was not only women, but men too who needed to respond in greater numbers to the threat of war.

Yet there were, in fact, many strenuous attempts to stop the war by the Women's International League for Peace and Freedom (WILPF), as outlined in the previous chapter, as well as by Pax International, the National Peace Council, the Peace Pledge Union, the largely working-class women's Co-operative Guild, and various religious groups. But there was little coherence and considerable confusion among peace activists in the late 1930s, chiefly because of the increasingly difficult conflict between advocates of absolute pacifism and those who recognized the threat of fascist Germany (Liddington 1989, 148). Before the war what women would have needed to show was the *international* significance of women's inferior status and the way in which this status affected political relations between countries. What was required was a *united* international women's view. Women needed to solidify their political influence so that they could vitally affect the policies of their countries. The inequalities of women, economically and politically, in fascist, communist, and democratic countries made it impossible for them to limit national and international aggression, or even for a significant number of them to perceive it as a threat to themselves as women. Both before and during the war the WILPF did strive to educate women and men about economic, political, and psychological causes and effects of war and peace, as did other women's peace organizations. But not enough attention was given to women's inferior political status, as opposed to their social and economic inferiority, as the powerful obstacle preventing large numbers of international women from legislating peace. To combine humanism with international feminism was the political need and the practical difficulty.

Of course internationalism was a basic principle for the WILPF. During the war it maintained its head office in Geneva and stayed in contact with its members in every country where it was allowed a presence. Refugee members from Germany, Austria, Poland, and Czechoslovakia lived in Britain and participated in the league's British activities. Gertrude Baer, the German woman who played such an important role in the WILPF in Berlin until she was forced to leave the country in 1935, ran the league's New York office during the war. Tims says that in 1943 Baer submitted a proposal for a training center in internationalism, and had funds been available, the president of New York University would have supported the idea. Throughout the war the league endeavored to define constructive and workable peace aims (Bussey and Tims 1980, 171–172).[2] Trying to promote the concept of internationalism was an enormous and dangerous task for the league at a time when Britain had been inspired by Churchill's rhetoric to fight to protect itself no matter what the cost.

Thousands of women had had to live as best they could with the grave war losses they had sustained only twenty years before. And now they were being asked to sacrifice and to suffer another, far more deadly war, to put in jeopardy a second world they had built up of careers, family love and joy. Many of the women like Helena Swanwick, Maude Royden, and Vera Brittain, who had written and lectured against war for over twenty years—because the Great War had taken "our youth," "our joy," our "all we had"—no doubt felt in near despair that their struggles had been in vain; their life's work a seeming failure. Yet it was the pacifist Maude Royden who voiced the moral dilemma that fascism presented for pacifist feminists and others when she said, upon renouncing her pacifist belief in 1939: "The unbelievable thing had happened—there had come into the world something that was worse than war" (Oldfield 1989, 64). There were other well-known women whose pacifism retreated in the face of the fascist threat.[3] Virginia Woolf who was certainly a pacifist from 1929 onward, when she later published *Three Guineas*, gave up her pacifism for instance. We will return to Woolf later. We must not forget that the history of peacemakers was also made by men. The first English-speaking peace societies arose directly after the Napoleonic wars, even though governments then regarded war, or the threat of war, as a normal right of policy-making. Bertrand Russell, for instance, was imprisoned for his pacifist views in 1918. An article by Bertram Pinkard on "Friends and the Organization of Peace," published in *The Friend* for 19 March 1961, described the century and a half since 1815 as though divided by a watershed—by World War I and the League of Nations. After the foundation of the league, governments began to agree that war should be ended rather than modified, and they undertook, at least in theory, to renounce their freedom to make war. But all this changed with the advent of fascist Germany; and when, in 1933, Hitler took over the Saarland and withdrew from the League of Nations, all real hope of peace died. Nazism produced two distinctly different kinds of pacifism, one antifascist, the other "a new pacifism" involving a personal commitment not to condone or support war.

At about this time, in 1936, Dick Sheppard, an Anglican minister, founded the Peace Pledge Union, whose credo was an uncompromising pacifism inspired by the power of the Cross to turn hate into love. These pacifists sought to mitigate the peculiar cruelties of World War II, such as obliteration bombing and large-scale starvation on the blockaded continent of its weakest inhabitants: children, the old, and the sick. They also helped, whenever opportunity offered, to care for refugees and for the victims of internment camps. Vera Brittain joined the Peace Pledge Union when, soon after its formation, it was opened to women (Liddington 1989, 158).

Many women were profoundly distrustful of the government that had seemed to want a peaceful democracy as expressed in its efforts at the League of Nations, yet had failed to prevent war.

But in the increasingly effective war propaganda campaign of 1939, war protests were not popular, and when war was declared, the majority of women accepted it; they were in "for the duration." Like World War I, the Second World War brought the issues of sexual discrimination and women's rights to the centre of the political stage. And in both wars the lives and moral attitudes of millions of women and men underwent extensive trauma, radically changing each one's image of self in marriage, in the workplace, in the family, and in society.

Women's Groups at the Outbreak of War

At the outbreak of war there were some women's groups other than the organized peace groups, but initially these groups were not prepared for war. The National Council of Women had a membership of about 13,000 made up mostly of middle- and upper-middle-class women, and the National Federation of Women's Institutes, founded in 1915 to help in the production and preservation of food, had a membership of about 338,000 country women concerned mostly with women's housewifely duties. The National Union of Townswomen's Guilds, founded in 1933, was the town equivalent of the Women's Institutes, and had about 10,000 members in 1939. "Each of these organizations noted a feeling of paralysis amongst their members at the outbreak of war. Branch secretaries left to do war work; local halls were commandeered by the military, by ARP (Air Raid Precautions) authorities, by evacuated children. Office staffs were reduced, premises cut down, publications appeared drastically diminished in size" (Sheridan 1991, 75). But this was at the very beginning of the war, sometimes called the "phony" war, between September 1939 and May 1940. After this time nearly every woman in the land, except for the convinced pacifists, worked for the war effort in many different ways.

Women in the Armed Services: A Brief Outline

As we shall see, women's experience on the home front during World War II was in many respects vastly different from that of women in World War I; the second war was far less exclusively a male operation. The women who served in the armed services also underwent a different experience.

   With the passing of the National Service Act in Great Britain in December 1941 young women (if unmarried or childless widows) became liable—for the first time in British history—for compulsory service with the Armed Forces or for other forms of national service. A royal proclamation later extended this to women between the ages of nineteen and thirty, although in practice only those born between 1918 and 1923 were called up. Women had the same right to appeal on the grounds of conscientious objection as men. However, although the National Service Act made women liable to conscription, one real difference remained in the liabilities of the two sexes, for the act provided that no woman called up for service should actually be required to use any lethal weapon or even take part in its use, without her written consent. One exception was the Special Operations Executive (SOE) a British organization that organized and coordinated Resistance operations in German-occupied territory. The work was secret and hazardous.[4] SOE women were treated exactly like men and suffered the highest proportion of casualties of all women who served in the war.

   In the army women drove lorries and ambulances and maintained their own vehicles, which was heavy, dirty work. They also prepared blood for the Army Transfusion Service. Some of the Equipment Units in the Air Force were run entirely by the Women's Auxiliary Air Force (WAAF). In the War Office Signal Office women dealt with important operational communications from every part of the world where there were British troops. During the invasion of France, members of the WAAF and Women's Royal Naval Service (WRNS) worked on teleprinters, operating 200-line switchboards and deciphering messages. WRNS were trained in semaphore, wireless telegraphy, ciphers and codes.

   The WAAF played a vital role in signalling. During the initial stages of the invasion of Europe in June 1944 more than two thousand airwomen worked the greatest signals communication system ever assembled. Teleprinters transmitted nearly one million words a day to British and American fighter units. The duties of Searchlight Batteries included using their light beams to guide home pilots in difficulties. The work needed much technical knowledge and ability to operate delicate instruments. This work in the later stages of the war was entirely in the hands of the women of the Auxiliary Territorial Service (ATS). Most of the battle of the Atlantic was plotted day-by-day by the WRNS; they knew the location of most ships afloat. Photography also plays an important part in air operations, and the women in the WAAF developed and also plotted night photos taken by bomber crews over their targets. They were also involved in the analysis of air reconnaissance photos. Constance Babington Smith, who found the V1 rocket site at Peenemünde on a photo, was the most famous of this group of women.

The present feminist debate on the militarization of women has a respectable history, but it does not take sufficiently into account the fact that many women, both in the Allied forces and in Germany, were aggressive supporters of both world wars. As we all know, militarism is essentially antifeminist, but not all women are anti-militarist.[5] Furthermore, women were con-scripted into the services and into war work by the government, and to disobey involved stiff financial penalties and even impris-onment. Of course one can argue that this policy was also part of the "militarization" of women, that it was foisted upon them through no choice of their own. I would argue that it was women and men in Britain and Germany who together chose war, or rather allowed it to happen, whose failure to create a war-resisting psychology in the 1930s led to the devastation of World War II.

Women on the Home Front

From the very beginning the war presented women almost im-mediately, and far sooner than in the First World War, with acute, far-reaching problems. Not only were their husbands sent away to fight, but their children also were evacuated, or other parents' children were billeted with them. These tremendous upheavals in family life presented physical and psychic dislocations. Yet these women accepted the war as inevitable. Mass-Observation reported the remarks of a working-class woman who said: "I used to believe in God, but now I don't know I'm sure. Look at a man like Hitler. It does seem we've got to have a war" (Sheridan 1991, 73). The report goes on to say that "this is the type of woman, unattached to any organisation, at the mercy of rising prices and the hazards of employment—there has been a severe increase in unemployment amongst wage-earning and salaried women since August [1939]—who is bearing the brunt of this home-front war . . ." (ibid.). The blackout was another important factor increasing nervous tension in women. The only good thing to come out of these early and painful upheavals the war caused in women's lives was that the evacuation policy aroused the nation's conscience, for it revealed conditions of social deprivation endured by much of the population of the industrial inner city areas, both in the north and south of the country.

In addition to the difficulties of evacuation and its associated problems, women had to try and deal with many other new pressures after war was declared, such as the emotional stress of the physical breakup of the family and the underlying fear for husbands, sons, brothers. Conscription had also increased the economic difficulties of the housewife, creating a situation where she was left to provide for her children and keep her home going with inadequate support from military allowances. For a married woman with two children the wife's allowance was twenty-five shillings a week, whereas her husband may have been earning three times as much before entering the service. In the army he earned £20 a month. Perhaps the best way of summing up the impact of the first year of war on the lives of women on the home front is to quote Mass-Observation again:

> Compulsion is often disguised as voluntary action, in which women are experiencing the greatest changes in their lives that they could ever imagine; the woman in the home is undergoing much that is difficult and undermining to health and morale; evacuation, conscription, air-raids, the struggle to live, the need to work—all these things are making an indelible effect on her mind, determining her outlook and attitude to everything from rationing to religion, from leisure habits to death. (Sheridan 1991, 93)

In wartime the family is not simply a biological unit, but one fostered and at times manipulated by the state, which takes on the role of the absent father so that personal, social, and political categories seem to merge more dramatically than in peacetime.

Prewar Women Workers

Here we might think for a moment about the majority of working women who entered the pre-World War II workforce: they were, in general, unmarried, under thirty-five, and by tradition, paid less than half the male rate. Women were denied entry into much heavy industrial work, and in the factories where they did work, they were not allowed to do overtime, and they could not work on Sundays; they were also prohibited from doing night work. Many feminists suspected that such regulations, ostensibly passed to protect the female labor force from an unhealthy working environment, were really a way of reducing women's industrial wage, since they excluded women from the high-paying industries of steel and heavy engineering (J. Lewis 1984, 56).

The "marriage bar" applied not only to women in industry, but to women in the professions of teaching and the civil service, local and national. Notwithstanding the 1919 Sex Disqualification Removal Act, which in theory had opened up all the professions except the top grades of the civil service, women remained predominantly at the bottom of the career ladder and the salary scale in the civil service and in teaching. Although it was not easy for women to enter the professions of medicine and the law, however they did receive equal pay once they got in.

Women Munition Workers

In the state-run munitions factories during the first months of the war neither equal pay nor much employment were offered the daughters of the women who had packed shells with the cordite that stained hands and faces yellow in World War I. An article in the *Evening News* of 15 September 1939, entitled "Women Will Feed the Guns Again," reminded these same daughters that their mothers had worked ten hours a day from the spring of 1915 onward. It made the point that once again the services of women munition workers would be in demand, earlier than they had been in the First World War. The article continues with the pro-feminist statement about those women's worth, ignoring the fact that the majority of them were forced to leave their jobs in 1919 and return to domestic life:

> To watch young girls hard at work for ten hours a day on filling shells, lubricating bullets, handling cordite, making, inspecting and gauging fuses, examining work where the thousandth part of an inch was vital, . . . spending their days in the unaccustomed surroundings of high explosives with as little fuss as if they were knitting socks, was a sight that many anti-feminists must have found encouraging. (London *Evening News*, 15 Sept. 1939)

The writer, Evelyn Irons, goes on to make the point that in the winter of 1939 many people—"mostly men"—seem to believe that women have "snapped up all the jobs vacated by men called to military duty, as well as cornering all new branches of our war effort, from the censorship to driving lorries, or chauffeuring staff officers in luxurious cars." Yet the figures for unemployed women in November 1939 leapt by 174,981 from the previous month's total. To deal with one aspect of the problem at this early stage in the war, the Women's Engineering Society took it upon themselves to form a deputation to go to Parliament and lay before women M.P.s a statement of their case (Costello 1985, 199). This slow start to women's wartime employment changed during the acute national emergency that arose after Hitler's divisions were threatening to conquer Europe in May 1940, although the question of equal pay for women was a focal point of women's agitation for the whole period of the war. The war could not have been fought without the vital contribution made by women, but once again, as in World War I, they were not politically well enough organized to obtain economic gains. In other words, women did not sufficiently define themselves as a single workforce to bargain with. The women of Britain recognized their obligation to the state in wartime, but the obligation of the state to women citizens was never fully acknowledged as far as equal pay went. Women in the civil service fared no better than women factory workers. They were forced to resign when they got married, but because of the national emergency they were "allowed back" at a far lower rate of pay.

As late as December 1943, the secretary of the Six Point Group had written to the International News protesting against the necessity for women to obtain their husbands' permission prior to taking paid employment (Fawcett Library Archives). The postwar downgrading of the economic status of working women was a repetition of what had happened after World War I.[6] In 1919, the leaders of the suffragette movement had tried to link voting rights to equal pay and equal opportunity, but the right to vote was a relatively easier goal to achieve. What was desperately needed after World War II were more women in Parliament to structure and legislate the economic, social, and political lives of women.[7] In the general election of July 1945, the first since 1935, of the eighty-seven women candidates twenty-four were elected, representing 3.8 percent of the total members of Parliament. Clearly, women needed to prepare themselves in every way to play a more representative part in government.

Women's War Work from 1940

Women's war work was soon to be of the utmost importance. Across the Channel in late May 1940, a vast human and military disaster was in the making. "Along the canals of Northern France, from Nieuport to Seclin, from Carvin to Gravelines, the 390,000 men of General Lord Gort's British Expeditionary Force [BEF], the Belgians and the French First Army gripped tight on their rifles and waited" (Collier 1980, 101). Retreat was inevitable. Anthony Eden, the secretary for war, had that very morning authorized a retreat of the entire British army to the coast. On the outskirts of Ronecq, Captain Harry Smith roused his sleeping company to give them the incredible news: "We are making a general retreat to the coast . . . The idea is to get back to England so we can return to France later" (102). In replying to Eden's command, Lord Gort had sent his own version of the retreat; he cabled London: "I must not conceal from you that a great part of B.E.F. and its equipment will inevitably be lost" (101). That "great part" was miraculously, unbelievably, small.

At this crucial time for Britain's survival, a major shift in government policy was necessary; a vital need had arisen to rearm Britain's miraculously rescued army after its nightmare defeat at Dunkirk, where it had left most of its heavy weapons on the beaches and in the surrounding fields. The Admiralty's last order to the navy sent to rescue the BEF was "Mind you bring back the guns." If Britain was to be the last line of defense, even rifles might soon be at a premium. Churchill emphasized that Dunkirk was not to be thought of as a victory, it was a defeat; albeit one in which the brave sailors of that famous armada of nearly a thousand ships of all classes had courageously and incredibly rescued 338,226 men. Of those left in France, forty thousand had been taken prisoner of war (with a long five years of internment ahead of them), and twenty-eight thousand had lost their lives. Churchill's speech directly after Dunkirk shows him clearly warning of the possibility of invasion, "We shall not flag or fail. We shall go on to the end, . . . we shall defend our island whatever the cost may be, we shall fight on the beaches, we shall fight on the landing-grounds, we shall fight in the fields and in the streets, we shall fight in the hills; we shall never surrender. . . ." (*Their Finest Hour*, 1962, 102).

For many anxious women and men a German invasion was a terrifying probability. Virginia Woolf's husband, Leonard, wrote that he and his friends had provided themselves with poison should the Germans arrive in England. Other citizens were busily reading the pamphlet issued by the Ministry of Information in cooperation with the War Office and the Ministry of Home Security, "If The INVADER Comes—What To Do—And

How To Do It." The introduction to the seven rules of what to do began: "The Germans threaten to invade Great Britain. If they do they will be driven out by our Navy, our Army, and our Air Force. Yet the ordinary men and women of the civilian population will also have their part to play." The rules included not panicking and taking to the roads with all portable possessions, as the tragic refugees of France, Holland, and Belgium had recently done, thus blocking the roads and exposing themselves to merciless machine-gun fire. "IF THE GERMANS COME BY PARACHUTE, AEROPLANE OR SHIP, YOU MUST REMAIN WHERE YOU ARE. THE ORDER IS 'STAY PUT.'" The seventh and last rule is revealing in its implied attitude toward the individual: "THINK BEFORE YOU ACT. BUT THINK ALWAYS OF YOUR COUNTRY BEFORE YOU THINK OF YOURSELF."

Churchill's famously defiant artillery of words, "blood, toil, sweat and tears," intensified the "Dunkirk spirit" and helped concentrate labor production into an immense war effort. Until he became prime minister in May 1940 there was no redistribution of women's labor. Now, under government policy, many "inessential" factories were closed for the duration. These factories for products such as shoes, paper, textiles, clothing, and hosiery had employed high proportions of women who now put their hands to work heavy presses, lathes, and drills that forged the weapons needed by their men if Britain was to withstand the dreadful probability of a Nazi invasion.

In the dire national emergency after Dunkirk, women joined the rapidly expanding workforce producing tanks and guns for the army and fighter planes for the RAF. At the height of the manpower crisis in 1943, the percentage of women in Britain's engineering industry rose to 31 percent, later this was to fall back to 13 percent after the war, when thousands of women, some of them with the utmost reluctance to give up the independence and interest in life war work had afforded them, were driven back into domesticity.

Until 1941 war work for women remained voluntary. As discussed earlier, women could, and did, enroll in the women's sections of the forces: the Auxiliary Territorial Service (ATS), the Women's Royal Naval Service (WRNS), and the Women's Auxiliary Air Force (WAAF). They could also care for the sick in many of the nursing services or work on the land. In March 1941 the basis of women's voluntary war work shifted when labor shortages were becoming serious. The government wanted to mobilize the female labor force more fully but was afraid of public reaction, so it tried to achieve its goal without direct compulsion by inviting women to register at employment exchanges; this actually gave the Minister of Labour the power to send anyone in the country anywhere to perform such services.

The Women's Consultative Committee, which included two women M.P.s, Dr. Edith Summerskill (Labour) and Irene Ward (Conservative), together with representatives of national women's organizations and unions, operated under the chairmanship of Ernest Bevin's parliamentary secretary. The purpose of the committee was to advise on wartime recruiting from the women's point of view, and although only consultative, it asked such questions as: Should a young married woman without children be treated differently from a single woman? Is a woman's marital status of significance? The committee also played a part in shaping the "voluntary" practice of asking all single women aged twenty to twenty-one who were without household responsibilities and full-time employment to register at government employment agencies as "mobile" labor—to be directed to filling vacancies in "essential war factories" (Brookes 1967, 137–139).

Conscription of Women into Armaments

The voluntary principle was abandoned altogether in December 1941. The Minister of Labour, Ernest Bevin, was forced to acknowledge that conscription of women was necessary. Women were desperately needed to replace men in the factories and in the support services of the military. With the exception of mothers of children under fourteen and certain women running households and taking care of other war workers, the National Service Act (No. 2) conscripted single women between the ages of twenty (later lowered to nineteen) and thirty. In other words, from January 1942 the government effectively instituted a limited but nationwide mobilization of women who were by law required to make themselves available for "vital war work" or, as auxiliaries, to make up the recruiting shortfalls, which had been falling behind the monthly targets by thirty thousand. The list of occupations defined as "vital" included work in munition factories, civil defense, nursing, the Women's Land Army, aircraft manufacture, the Royal Observer Corps, the radio industry, tank manufacture, and the transport industry. Women who refused to register and obey these government laws were liable to be fined up to five pounds a day and even imprisoned.

By the middle of 1943 the labor crisis in the factories had become so severe that the government stopped recruiting for the women's armed forces for twelve months. Womanpower was directed to the factories. The only alternative to factory work was work on the land, producing the nation's food.

The Women's Land Army was the only women's civilian service under the direct control of the government. The women had a marching song, "Back to the land, we must lend a hand, / To the farms and the fields we must go." Few of the thousands who eventually joined up to "do their bit with a hoe" regarded it as a soft option. Wearing green sweaters, dungarees, and boots, these young women worked a forty-eight-hour week for thirty-five shillings, of which twenty to twenty-five shillings went in board and lodging. They were given seven days paid holiday a year, whereas women in the forces were given twenty-eight. The work was arduous; healthy, but no country picnic. By the end of the war the country owed them an incalculable debt.

The conscription of women necessarily involved an acceptance of the same problems faced by women who undertook the dual role of unpaid domestic work and paid industrial work, which imposed a double burden on the women. A change in social attitudes towards the employment of women was essential. In the period before the war, a middle-class woman who married and decided to continue to work was often subject to extreme social pressures and had to go deliberately against the prevailing ethos. Her husband, too, might not have wanted her to work, convinced that her work stigmatized him as a man who could not financially support his family. Even some leaders of working-class women's groups agreed that a wife's wages might deter the husband from finding work (J. Lewis 1984, 51). As Pat Ayers points out, it is important to realize that for working-class women the freedom to work outside the home was a form of emancipation that until now they had readily given up.

> Practically all working class girls are compelled to earn their living in the interval between school and marriage; for them paid work has not been a symbol of emancipation but a stern and often regretted necessity. The woman wage-earner has not looked upon her industrial occupation as a career, nor as an opportunity to express her individuality, nor as the means of providing herself with an honourable alternative to marriage. Neither the types of work in which women have been employed, nor the wages and conditions afforded them, have been such as to cast any glamour over earning a living.

When marriage, home and children offered themselves as an alternative, industrial work could be sacrificed without a pang. (1988, 24)

The government therefore had to change public attitudes as well as the women's own attitudes and convince these now vital workers that their duty lay not in their homes, as previously presumed, but in the country's war efforts to increase arms production. In other words, the state was forced into an acceptance that the roots of economic and social disadvantage from which women suffered might be found in the dual role they play in society as mothers and workers. Many of society's attitudes changed radically during the war; yet some were reversed after the war, suggesting once again, as in World War I, that really the nation wanted the women to change their roles only for the duration. Thus there was a certain impermanence about the transformation of women's social roles during wartime. Still, conscription into fulltime work during the war gave women more confidence in themselves and in their abilities and made them more articulate in their demands. This change in women's perception of themselves helped bring about greater political, social, and economic equality, if only gradually, in the postwar years. Many of these women and their daughters eagerly joined the women's movement of the 1960s and 1970s.

Women in the London Blitz

The German air assault of Britain began in June 1940, first over the Channel and the south coast, then over the southern counties and air force bases, and suddenly over London. On 7 September at 5 P.M. when the air-raid sirens wailed out their warning, Londoners were slow to believe they were under attack, little realizing that this raid was the first of fifty-seven consecutive nights of raids to come. By 8 P.M. on this apocalyptic night of the blitz so early in the war, it seemed as if the whole city was in flames. The terrifying and uninhibited violence went on all winter.

After losing the Battle of Britain in the summer of 1940, the Germans switched from daylight to night attacks, continuing this policy all winter long, also devastating cities such as Coventry and Birmingham. Collier (1980, 257) reports that between 7 September and 13 November 1940, 13,651 tons of high explosives and 12,586 incendiary canisters hit London. The worst and last assault came on 10 May 1941, when thousands of high explosive and incendiary bombs fell on the city, lighting more than two thousand fires and, by smashing a hundred and fifty or so water mains when the Thames was at low tide, made it impossible to put out the fires, they went on burning for days. By the time of this last Luftwaffe assault 51,000 tons of high explosives had fallen on London alone. Mercifully, although there were sporadic attacks on London after May 1941, the German air force was not to return in large numbers until February 1944, when London was again attacked, with flying-bombs and rockets. In the twelve months from June 1940 to June 1941 the civilian casualties were 43,381 killed and 50,856 seriously injured, a total of 94,237 (Churchill 1962, 39–40). These deaths exceed those of British military personnel up to that time.

The saying "A woman's place is in the home" took quite a beating one way and another during World War II. During the blitz, home became one of the most dangerous and devastating places to be. As well as their war work, the civilian population—mostly women, children, middle-aged men, the aged and infirm—had to face the terror of the barbaric nightly bombing attacks on their cities and homes. The nightly descent into the shelters, whether the large public ones of places like London and Liverpool, or the family-sized "Anderson" buried four feet deep in private gardens, were an immense trial for everyone. Part of the terror was in only partly knowing what was going on.

The public shelters were overcrowded, gritty from broken sandbags, foul smelling, with very few lavatories, and rat-infested. By the end of September 1940, 177,000 forlorn figures were sleeping in the London Underground, where their shadows rose above them, casting huge forms on the white-tiled walls. Yet there was a vast impressiveness about the defenseless huddles of citizens that inspired many, including the artist Henry Moore, who sketched some of them as emblems of stoical family endurance under attack. Although the majority of Londoners sought refuge at home in the Andersons in their own gardens, the London Underground, sheltering thousands, has become the symbol of the blitz. And the blitz itself, like the military defeat at Dunkirk, has become a powerful part of the mythos of World War II.

Life was hellishly unnatural; even the confused birds sang all night long as the intense brightness of the searchlights turned night into day (Collier 1980, 256). In the mornings after all-night raids, many weary families would trudge home, only to find it a smoldering pile of bricks and wood. The homeless women and children were faced with salvaging from the rubble what they could—the odd photograph, a battered saucepan, a child's toy perhaps—and then urgently trying to find a new home. This usually turned out to be a public housing shelter, a church or school hall, and not always in the same district that the family had been living in, so that ration cards had to be changed, a new school found for the children, new everything had to be acquired in fact—clothes, furniture, toys. (Not all children were evacuated, and of those who were, some did not remain so for the duration.) By May 1941 tens of thousands of people had lost their homes, and over a million houses were damaged.

The Women's Voluntary Service (WVS) played a vital role in relieving some of the social misery and suffering of the blitz. They were the largest group of volunteer women from all classes and all ages, but especially from the age group too old to be conscripted for "official" war work. They worked against great odds: inadequate funds and supplies, lack of training, and long hours with insufficient sleep (Minns 1980, 65–73). The women of the WVS dealt compassionately and efficiently with all manner of tragic problems, such as cooking for those who had been bombed out, sorting out personal belongings, and helping to identify fatalities. Their contribution to the war effort was immeasurable. After a raid, to the immense joy of being alive was often added the harrowing fear of having lost one's home. The aim of this sort of bombing was in fact to demoralize the British and induce them to surrender; but groups like the WVS played an immensely important part in meliorating the planned demoralization by their unfailing devotion to the social and psychological needs of helpless victims of the blitz. In fact, bombing as a morale-breaker was a failure both in Britain and in Germany.

British and German Women Writing on the War: The Blitz of Berlin

The terror and mass destruction caused by the German blitzkrieg on Britain has its appalling parallel in the so-called "precision bombing" of Germany in 1943–45, which exacted far more senseless destruction and suffering than even the citizens of Britain had had to endure. Vera Brittain was one woman pacifist writer who vehemently opposed mass bombing, and she devoted much time to writing and publishing her views, particularly in her 1944 book, *Seeds of Chaos*. Her "Lament for Cologne" (published in *The Friend*, 19 June 1943) also expresses the anguished outrage of mothers who are forced to witness the destruction of their homes, their families, and their communities. The remedy is a call for all women, British and German, to unite and stop such barbaric action. The poem has an historical double edge to it for Brittain had visited Cologne in 1924 and witnessed the abjectness of its citizens and their starvation and unemployment as a result of the Allied blockade of Germany and the demand for war reparations.

> Perhaps, when passions die and slaughters cease,
> The mothers on whose homes destruction fell,
> Who wailing sought their children through the hell
> Of London, Warsaw, Rotterdam, Belgrade,
> Will seek Cologne's sad women, unafraid,
> And cry: "God's cause is ours. Let there be peace!"
>
> (1944, 134)

But outrage is not enough, the poet suggests; international women must use these feelings to move them to action. Both sides of the conflict must work together, must cooperate to create a peace-keeping mentality in women and men, as well as in their leaders. Peace workers should work not just for their families but for their communities both local and international, and to do this requires being politically aware and organized. Governments, as we know, cannot make war without the help of women. Women are asked to serve in wartime and to prepare for war, but if women worked instead to prepare conditions in which war would not occur, then war might cease to be the policy option it has always been. Throughout the war, Vera Brittain tried to show that the immense effort going into the war ought to have been used to produce peace.

In August of 1943 the growing horror of the air war over Germany surpassed all powers of imagination, and still there seemed to be no diminishment in the power of its citizens to endure such unmitigated violence. As in Britain, the effect upon German citizens of mass bombing was not anger and revolt, but apathy and fatigue, and a mechanical endeavor to save what could be saved. Moreover, it was no doubt difficult for the victims of such concentrated bombing to give in since they were ruled by the iron fist of the Gestapo. In *Seed of Chaos*, Brittain writes that Hamburg had the equivalent ("so we are told") of sixty Coventries. She goes on to say that she, among many others, went to Coventry shortly after the raid on 14 November 1940, and saw for herself what "the cruel attack meant to a once historic city and its inhabitants" (Brittain 1944, 35). She asks if the inhabitants of Coventry really enjoy the thought that the citizens of Hamburg, "the most anti-Nazi city in the Reich," suffered sixty times as much as they did. "Does it really fill them with glee to reflect that sixty times their number of children, expectant mothers, women in childbirth, invalids, and aged people have perished in terror and anguish?" (35).

Some of them had already made it clear that it did not. Brittain quotes a letter in the *New Statesman*, 30 November 1940:

> Sir,
>   Many citizens of Coventry who have endured the full horror of an intense aerial bombardment would wish to dispute statements made in the Daily Express to the effect that all people of Coventry expressed the opinion that they wished to bomb, and bomb harder, the peoples of Germany. . . . (36)

Writing at the end of 1943, Brittain claims that the vengeful sentiments referred to in that letter are still felt by many British people; but they either do not know the facts about mass bombing, or they have consciously "put shutters over the window of their imagination" (37). She also asserts that many "deliberately turn their backs upon knowledge, ashamed and fearful of accepting the realities which a determined facing of the facts would disclose" (37). She then spends the rest of her book giving the facts culled from the British press and that of neutral countries.

Of course, some of these reports will be more accurate than others, and the aims of propaganda must also be taken into account; nevertheless, these newspaper reports represent the information the British public was given and are therefore a considerable source for the formation of public opinion on mass bombing, or precision and saturation bombing. The German expression, Marie Vassiltchikov tells us, was *Bombenteppich* [bomb carpet] (1987, 106). This expression is certainly less hard to swallow than the dreadful ironies of "precision bombing." Brittain outlines the fate of Germany's capital city, Berlin, under what by 1944 had come to be called by many "obliteration bombing." German propaganda called it, not unjustifiably, "terror bombing." *The Daily Telegraph* gave the "fullest and most comprehensive" details of the "historic" raid on Berlin of 24 November 1943, describing it as "very nearly the heaviest raid on any target in the history of air warfare" (43). The account continued:

"Reports from neutral capitals last night made it clear that the havoc was on an unprecedented scale, particularly in the centre of the city. Thousands were reported killed and injured. . . . Unbroken heavy cloud lay along the route. . . . We bombed Berlin blind. The bombers followed the brightly lit 'target indicators' although the target area itself was not seen" (43). On 25 November after the third heavy raid, The Daily Telegraph reported: "The fire brigades and A.R.P. personnel are powerless to cope with the situation. Day has turned to night by the billowing clouds of evil-smelling smoke which fill the streets. . . . Unter den Linden is a shambles to-day, there are long lines of burning buildings in it . . . The University State Library is burning" (44).

Between 18 November and 4 January more than fourteen thousand tons of bombs were dropped on Berlin. Brittain reports that on Christmas Eve 1943 a heavy raid was launched at 4 A.M. On 4 January 1944, The News Chronicle, according to Brittain, disclosed a calculation by Bomber Command that another fifteen to twenty more big attacks would be needed "to finish the job." The previous Sunday, 2 January, the air correspondent of The Observer had remarked that "it will probably not be necessary to devastate more than 12,000 of Berlin's vital 18,000 acres to end its wartime life as an organized city." The article continued: "Some of the districts known to have been bombed are among the most densely populated in Europe" (48).

Concluding her book, Brittain writes that it is difficult to estimate the amount of public misgiving that exists on the subject of obliteration bombing. She mentions a "valuable article" published 12 February 1944 in the New Statesman by Mass-Observation on vengeance. The article testifies to the divided mind of many British citizens on "reprisals" and to a considerable amount of uneasiness about the bombing. She quotes Mass-Observation: "It was regularly found, that, after a blitz, people in bus, street, and pub seldom talked of getting their own back," and "nearly every one in four expresses feelings of uneasiness or revulsion about Britain's present methods of bombing" (97). Brittain goes on to say that in compiling her book she found it difficult to find printed expressions of concern, which she maintains were officially discouraged. The few letters that did appear in the press, she thinks, are probably unrepresentative of the number received. But she did find one in the New Statesman's rival, The Spectator, 24 September 1943:

Why is it that so many religious leaders, politicians and journalists who denounced German barbarism during the heavy raids on this country, now either applaud such methods when they are adopted in intensified form by the Allies, or acquiesce by their silence? (97)

And still the bombing went on, directed by Air Marshall Arthur Harris, Chief of Bomber Command, culminating in the appalling destruction of Dresden on 13 February 1945 when, in a single night, thirty-five thousand people were killed.[8]

Marie "Missie" Vassiltchikov's *Berlin Diaries* provide us with an eye witness account of the saturation bombing of Berlin. As a young refugee Russian aristocrat, living and working with her colleagues and friends among the ruins of the city, she—just like the British under aerial bombardment—showed enormous courage and the sort of endurance to carry on that defeats all the aims of this sort of warfare. Of the raid on Tuesday, 23 November 1943, she records in her diary: "Last night the greater part of central Berlin was destroyed. . . . We had hardly got there [shelter] when we heard the first approaching planes. They flew very low and the barking of the flak (antiaircraft guns) was suddenly drowned by a very different sound, that of exploding bombs, first far away and then closer and closer, until it seemed as if they were falling literally on top of us. . . . The planes did not come in waves, as they do usually, but kept on droning ceaselessly overhead" (Vassiltchikov 1987, 106). The aftermath was even more devastating, for the wind had suddenly risen and the fires were spreading. "We all went out into our little square and, sure enough, the sky on three sides was blood-red . . . the greatest danger would come in a few hours' time when the fire storm really got going" (107). Yet, after the raid of 24 November she reports that "the sight of those endless rows of burnt-out or still burning buildings had got the better of me and I was beginning to feel panicky. The whole district, many of its houses so familiar to me, had been wiped out in just one night!" On Wednesday, 24 November, she tells of a friend who staggered out into the devastated streets still enveloped in thick smoke—"ashes rained down" (109)—and stumbled into a grimy-faced old woman, whom she suddenly realized was her own eighty-year-old mother. She had been walking the streets trying to reach her daughter after her own flat had been completely burnt out. "Missie" describes the scene as she found it that morning:

The instant I left the house I was enveloped in smoke and ashes rained down on my head. I could breathe only by holding a handkerchief to my mouth and blessed Heinz for lending me those goggles. . . . As I continued down Lützowstrasse the devastation grew worse; many buildings were still burning and I had to keep to the middle of the street, which was difficult on account of numerous wrecked trams. There were many people in the streets, most of them muffled in scarves and coughing, as they threaded their way gingerly through the piles of fallen masonry. At the end of Lützowstrasse, about four blocks away from the office, the houses on both sides of the street had collapsed and I had to climb over mounds of smoking rubble, leaking water pipes and other wreckage . . . Until then I had seen very few firemen around, but here some were busily trying to extricate people trapped in the cellars. On Lützowplatz all the houses were burnt out. The bridge over the river Spree was undamaged, but on the other side all the buildings had been destroyed. . . . A woman seized my arm and yelled that one of the walls was tottering and we both started to run. I caught sight of the mail box into which I had dropped that long letter to Tatiana the night before; it still stood but was completely crumpled. (109–10)

Yet, in spite of the colossal damage and danger, she went on bravely with her work and her commitment to that dedicated and heroic group of Germans who were plotting the assassination of Hitler.

A month before D-day, on 7 May 1944, Missie describes a massive raid while she was at mass.

By the time the service was over, I felt fifty years older and completely drained. Later I heard there had been fifteen hundred planes over Berlin that morning. In the early days of the war thirty seemed to us dangerous enough. . . . Later we walked about the centre of the town. Unter den Linden, Wilhemstrasse, Friedrichstrasse had all been badly hit. There was much smoke and many new craters, but American bombs—the Americans come during the day, the British at night—seem to cause less damage than the English ones. These explode horizontally, whereas the former go deeper, so that neighbouring buildings collapse less easily. (172)

We have another invaluable personal account of the bombing of Berlin in Christabel Bielenberg's book, *The Past Is Myself.* Bielenberg, an Englishwoman, married her German husband, Peter, in 1934. She lived through the war in Germany as a German citizen under the evils of Nazi rule and Allied bombings. Her book covers the years 1935–45. As she herself says in her foreword, disclaiming the academic method for her book: "I have one advantage perhaps over those whose knowledge must needs depend on documents: I am English; I was German, and above all I was there." She writes:

> The bombs fell indiscriminately on Nazis and anti-Nazis, on women and children and works of art, on dogs and pet canaries. New and more ravaging bombs—blockbusters and incendiaries, and phosphorous bombs which burst and glowed green and emptied themselves down the walls and along the streets in flaming rivers of unquenchable flame, seeping down cellar stairs, and sealing the exits to the air-raid shelters. . . . (1980, 127)

She comes to the same conclusion about public morale as Missie who experienced the same savage cruelty; though dulled by grief, physical exhaustion, and lack of food, the citizens of Berlin would not surrender.

In fact it would take the converging Allied and Russian armies to bring Germany to its knees. Many commentators agree that the Allied demand made at Casablanca in 1943 for the unconditional surrender of Germany reinforced the nation's determination to fight to the bitter end. No doubt in the minds of many was the memory of the punitive Versailles treaty of 1919 and the ignominy it had forced upon Germany. Bielenberg writes:

> I learned when I was in Berlin that those wanton, quite impersonal killings, that barrage from the air which mutilated, suffocated, burned and destroyed, did not so much breed fear and a desire to bow before the storm, but rather a certain fatalistic cussedness, a dogged determination to survive and, if possible, help others to survive, whatever their politics, whatever their creed. (127)

Of course the Nazis were adept at using propaganda in advertising, in education, and in war. The fight against democracy and civilized living was promulgated as much by propaganda as by bombs. For the Nazis realized that the majority of people will accept an idea if it is attached to a familiar belief. The belief they inculcated in their besieged, exhausted citizens even in late 1943–44 was that Germany was unconquerable. Propaganda notwithstanding, life in blitzed Berlin must have been full of misery, suffering, and terror.

Between November 1943 and March 1944 Berlin was bombed twenty-four times. The attacks grew more and more massive, involving a thousand planes dropping thousands of tons of bombs. But while Berlin was a burned-out, devastated ruin and thousands of its citizens were killed or wounded, with about one and a half million people left homeless, the city went on producing munitions and other war weapons. In the words of the historian Max Hastings, "In the operational sense, the Battle of Berlin was more than a failure. It was a defeat . . . Berlin won, it was just too tough a nut to crack" (Vassiltchikov 1987, 125). What Air Marshall Harris's "area bombing" (high altitude non-precision bombing) did was barbaric; moreover, it did not achieve its purpose.

Churchill records that when visiting bombed-out Londoners in the winter of 1940, he had been glad to hear them shout "Give it 'em back" and "Let them have it too." He continues: "I undertook forthwith to see that their wishes were carried out; and this promise was certainly kept." Writing after the war, how-ever, he sees "saturation bombing" from a different perspective:

> The debt was repaid tenfold, twentyfold, in the frightful routine bom-bardment of German cities, which grew in intensity as our air power developed, as the bombs became far heavier and the explosives more powerful. Certainly the enemy got it all back in good measure, pressed down and running over. Alas for poor humanity! (1962, 299)

It is difficult to compare the experience of Londoners in 1940–41 with that of the German ordeal of the last three years of the war. The Allied bombing was heavier in every way: thousands more planes, bigger explosives, day and night bombing of many nonmilitary targets. Writing in 1949, Churchill admits that "if the bombs of 1943 had been applied to the London of 1940, we should have passed into conditions which might have pulverised all human organisation" (ibid., 313).

The reaction of the majority of women munition workers mak-ing the bombs, guns, and planes, to Vera Brittain's critique of saturation bombing is largely and regrettably unrecorded. Prob-ably many thought, once war had come, that it was as absurd to resist it as to resist an erupting volcano. The horror had material-ized, and it had to be endured. Participation in bringing it to a quick end would seem a satisfying motive, even if it did involve compromises. Brittain would no doubt have reiterated some points she made in her fortnightly "Personal Letter to Peace-Lovers"—for instance, that "pacifism is not a political program, but a way of life. . . . it cannot be sincerely maintained in con-junction with armaments even for purposes of 'defence' . . . Hence the pacifists' task is not to provide schemes for outmaneu-vering Hitler by some species of pious ingenuity, but to win supporters for standards of conduct whose practice by even a substantial minority would revolutionise the world" (Fawcett Archive pamphlet 172.4; Issue No. 14, 11 Jan. 1940).

One person who did publicly criticise Brittain's booklet *Seed of Chaos* was George Orwell, who made the point that since pacifists had not succeeded in preventing the war, they must acquiesce in any excesses the makers of war choose. In *Testament of a Generation* Brittain replies that her main concern is with the moral deterioration involved when a nation commits itself to "unrestrained infliction of cruelty" (Berry and Bishop 1985, 245). After Hiroshima, she believed that such moral turpitude had created the climate of opinion that made that horror possible. Brittain's view has found very recent support from another intrepid commentator on the devastating horror of World War II. Fussell writes that "area bombing led inevitably, as intensification overrode scruples, to Hiroshima and Nagasaki" (Fussell 1989, 16).

In 1938 Virginia Woolf like Brittain had taken a moral and pacifist stand against the "making or improvement" of weapons of war, since she saw these as threatening individual freedom. In other words, in a world where the idea that each individual's right to freedom is supremely important, that idea would be vastly more significant than the making of bombs. In fact, in such a world bombs would be obsolete. This may sound naive, but if this simple belief were acted upon nationally and internationally, in public and private life, it might well prevent the aggressive destructiveness of war. And it is worth remembering that the private and public life are inseparably connected.

Virginia Woolf gave us a remarkable piece of writing on the terrors of being bombed. It is an artist's response to the terror of imminent personal destruction. In "Thoughts on Peace in an Air Raid" she describes her feelings as the deathly planes fly over her house in Sussex:

> The sound of sawing overhead has increased. All the searchlights are erect. They point at a spot exactly above this roof. At any moment a bomb may fall on this very room. One, two, three, four, five, six . . . the seconds pass. The bomb did not fall. But during those seconds of suspense all thinking stopped. All feeling, save one dull dread, ceased. A nail fixed the whole being to one hard board. The emotion of fear and of hate is therefore sterile, unfertile. Directly that fear passes, the mind reaches out and instinctively revives itself by trying to create. (1961, 211)

Earlier in the year of 1940 a bomb on Mecklenberg Square had shattered Leonard and Virginia Woolf's offices and the Hogarth Press; shortly afterward a bomb on Tavistock Square destroyed their former home. All this intense physical destruction of furniture, books, and buildings together with the fear of more bombings and even invasion no doubt contributed considerably to Virginia Woolf's despair and depression when, in the spring of 1941, she took her own life. She was very much a victim of the terrors of war.

Some Other Women Pacifist Writers of World War II

There were other women writers who were aware of the moral discrepancy between women's traditional roles as part creators and caretakers of the human race, and women as makers of vastly complex, destructive weapons. Here are the thoughts of one of them, entitled "Nella's Last War":

> We all came out from the canteen early, as the evening squad turned up well on time. . . . As I was getting my coat, a quiet tired voice asked for the one in charge, and when I went back I saw a haggard man in civvies, who had a suitcase. He wanted to sell Christmas decorations—folded paper-chains, awful-looking roses etc. He said he was a discharged soldier, and would have shown his papers. A cold chill seemed to blow on me. . . . The phrase, "discharged soldier," brought such visions of the last war's aftermath. We *must* have plans, water-tight plans, to avoid it after this war. *Surely*, if the countries of the world spent the same money on peace, for one year, as they do for war, it would be a help. I don't understand about "markets" and "economics"—I'm very dumb—but I know how I plan ahead and work in my own little sphere, so that things go fairly smoothly. (Cambridge Women's Peace Collective 1984, 145).

This was written on 4 December 1942 for Mass-Observation: Nella Last was one of their most conscientious observers; "one of the people;" she kept a diary of her life in Barrow, Lancashire, throughout the Second World War. On 19 August 1943 she wrote:

> Two women have sat side by side for years at the Centre, sewing at bandages. One has lost two sons at sea—and now learns her airman son has to be "presumed dead". Her daughter had to join the W.A.A.F. The other one's three sons work in the Yard—have good jobs—and the daughter of twenty-eight is "reserved", since she is

considered necessary as a secretary to a boss in the Yard. I look round the big room at faces I've known and loved for over four years. My heart aches and, even in that small circle, the bravery and courage, the "going on" when only sons have been killed, when letters don't come, when their boys are taught to fight like savages if they are commandoes—when they are trained, and trained and trained, for bodies to endure, and to go and kill other women's lads, to wipe all the light from other mother's faces. (ibid., 145–46)

Pacifist women like Helena Swanwick, Emily Hobhouse, Maude Royden, and Kate Courtney all argued in public during the First World War and wrote about the issue of the protector and the protected (see chapter 1). Virginia Woolf's polemic, *Three Guineas* (1938) warned about the seductiveness of the militarizing state in women's and children's lives, arguing that women must become "indifferent" to the blandishments of nationalism and militarism. In *Women Against the Iron Fist* (1989, 110), Sybil Oldfield introduces a little-known source of *Three Guineas*, which must have been Woolf's background thinking about war. Woolf kept a series of scrapbooks in the 1930s, selections of newspaper cuttings about contemporary Nazism, especially cuttings which emphasized Hitler's own abhorrent views: his militarism, masculinism, and antifeminism. As Woolf says in *Three Guineas*, centuries of dominance and acquiescence in that dominance have resulted in the maniacal masculine figure, "eyes glazed," his body "braced in an unnatural position," rigidly "cased in a uniform," "his hand is upon a sword" (1938, 217), or, one might add, hand on a gun or riding whip. "He is called in German and Italian Führer or Duce; in our own language Tyrant or Dictator. And behind him lie ruined houses and dead bodies—men, women and children" (217). But men and women between them have created "that figure," and together, by their thoughts and actions, they can "change that figure" (217). Like many writers before and after her, Woolf addresses herself to the behavior of war, to the psychology of the participants, and to the equation of domination with virility. In her end notes she quotes Julian Huxley, who "warns us that 'any considerable alteration of the hereditary constitution is an affair of millennia, not of decades.' On the other hand, as science also assures us that our life on earth is 'an affair of millennia, not of decades,' some alteration in the hereditary constitution may be worth attempting" (283–84). Oldfield interprets this to mean: "If 'male' could come to mean private nurturer and if 'female' could come to mean humane political decision-maker, then, Woolf suggests, there might still be hope" (Oldfield 1989, 121). Better still, I think, if these two states were equally interchangeable—so that some men could be nurturers, others politicians, and some women could be decision-making politicians whilst others could be caregivers, according to the individual woman or man's temperament and ability, as well as the needs of the community— then there would be justifiable hope for us all.

Woolf goes on to say that we can best prevent war not by repeating the mistakes of the past, but "by finding new words and creating new methods" and by working to realize that unity that "rubs out divisions as if they were chalk marks only;" so that the human spirit can "overflow boundaries and make unity out of multiplicity" (218). She admits this is an age-old dream of humanity, the "dream of peace," which cannot be realized while the sound of guns echoes around the world. Her ideas resemble those expressed by Freud in a letter to Einstein in 1932 that what will save us all from the murderous horrors of war is sinking our differences and recognizing all that unites us one to the other as individuals, groups and nations (Freud, 203–15). Woolf's millennial vision was irrelevant to the Europe of 1938: there was no way to be antifascist *and* antiwar. In the long term, however, her horror of war and her vision of the interconnectedness of all life, as expressed in her posthumously published novel, *Between the Acts* (which might have had as an alternative title, "Between the Wars") suggested valuable ideas for a shift in our psychology of war.

The vast majority of women were not pacifist, and many rallied to the call from Dr. Edith Summerskill, who, angry that women were denied the chance to join the Home Guard, formed the Women's Home Defence. These women met once a week to learn how to fire rifles, throw hand grenades, and deal with German parachutists. Naturally, the government encouraged this display of female militancy and arranged for regular army officers and for members of the Home Guard to be instructors.

In her fictionalized 1976 autobiography, *Kindheitmuster* (translated ironically as *A Model Childhood*, 1983), the German writer Christa Wolf, born in 1929, writes about the political and social forces that shaped her early life as a Nazi youth. It is a powerful book and an extraordinary testament of the way in which children growing up in a totalitarian, militarized state can be socialized from the start into conformity with its values. In Nazi Germany antinationalism was a crime, and obedience to the state was the chief means of self-esteem. Wolf was a youthful supporter of the Third Reich until the end of the war, when she was sixteen years old. The fact that the novel is a form of fictionalized autobiography suggests that even in 1976 the writer could not directly face her past; she could not face the painful knowledge of what she had been. She remembers, for example, her favorite teacher telling her that every good German girl must learn to hate. Her parents are implicated, too, in their compliance with the detestable regime. The book is a powerful statement about the emotional and intellectual damage the Nazis inflicted upon nearly all young Germans; it is also about the indelible effect the experience of such a regime had upon German identity, especially female identity, and the guilt that has left a permanent stain upon personality. Although the emotional trauma of such a childhood is lasting, Wolf fears that memory will be unreliable in constructing the history of her experience:

> Today you know that the honest word doesn't exist in the age of suspicion, because the honest speaker depends on an honest listener, and because the person who hears the distorted echo of his own words eventually loses his honesty. There's nothing he can do about it. We can no longer tell exactly what we have experienced. (362)

J. M. Ritchie writes that "It has often been claimed that there was no Nazi literature. A modification of this theory is the claim that Nazi literature did exist, but that most of it was written before 1933 and that the seizure of power and the creation of the *Reichsschrifttumskammer,* containing all literary production, meant the death of creative literature as such" (Ritchie, *Staging the War in German,* in Higgins 1986, 85).

In her second novel, *The Quest for Christa T.* (1982), Wolf, now in her early teens, reflects on her childhood past as she and her parents flee westwards from the advancing Russians, jammed into a small cabin of a munitions truck, one of the last vehicles to get away:

> Christa T., to ward off despair, pulls a child to her lap. Then the radio overhead begins to roar: once more, even in hell itself, this fanatical overplayed voice, loyalty, loyalty to the Führer, even unto death. But she, Christa T., even before she's understood the man, feels herself going cold. Her body, as usual, has understood before her brain has . . . There's a curse on the people sitting here and on me as well. Except she can't stand up any more when the song comes: there it is. I'm staying here. I'll hug this child . . . I'm not going to

raise my arm any more. I have the child, small warm breath. I won't sing the song with them any more. How they sing, . . . [they] stand up stiffly, pulled up straight by the song [Über alles in der Welt] . . . How shall we ever stand up straight again?" (19–20)

Christa Wolf, like Vera Brittain, advocates a constant humane awareness of the perilous influence that violence has upon the behavior of our children, ourselves, and society at large. If we can keep this perception of violence always before us, she suggests, we may be better able to resist the power of militarism in our lives. It may even be that the violence of war not only severs all our bonds of intimacy with others but that war actually arises out of a failure to make strong bonds in the first place.

Few of the courageous women whose efforts were so important during World War II had time to reflect on the larger significance of their contribution. Few asked, What does war mean? What will we do as survivors? How will we deal with tyranny in the future? How will we protect civilization and our children and their children from what Martha Gellhorn has called the cancer of war? For we have, she says, "learned no preventive medicine for the body of the nations. We fall back, again and again, on nearly fatal surgery" (1986, xi). It was only later that these questions were voiced for women by women writers. Writing is not only a war weapon but a peace weapon in the right hands.

Writing about the behavior that is war and its continuing ugly pattern in our lives, Margaret Mead expresses similar concern:

Warfare is here, as part of our thought; the deeds of warriors are immortalized in the words of our poets, the toys of our children are modeled upon the weapons of the soldier, the frame of reference within which our statesman and our diplomats work always contains war. If we know that it is not inevitable, that it is due to historical accident that warfare is one of the ways in which we think of behaving, are we given any hope by that? . . . 'Warfare is only an Invention—not a Biological Necessity.' (Mead, quoted in *My Country Is the Whole World*, Cambridge Women's Peace Collective 1984, 133–34)

These sentiments from Mead's autobiography of 1972 echo a much earlier peace activist, the Austrian Bertha von Suttner, who was the first woman to be given the Nobel Peace Prize, in 1905:

Since out of every scholar a defender of his country has to be formed, therefore the enthusiasm even of the child must be aroused for this its first duty as a citizen; his spirit must be hardened against the natural horror which the terrors of war might awaken, by passing over as quickly as possible the story of the most fearful massacres and butcheries as of something quite common and necessary, and laying meanwhile all possible stress on the ideal side of this ancient national custom; and it is in this way they have succeeded in forming a race eager for battle and delighting in war.

The girls—who indeed are not to take the field—are educated out of the same books as are prepared for the military training of the boys, and so in the female youth arises the same conception which exhausts itself in envy that they have nothing to do with war and in admiration for the military class. . . . War must be—it is the source of the highest dignities and honours—*that* the girls see very well, and they have had also to learn by heart the poems and tirades in which war is magnified. And thus originate the Spartan mothers, and the "mothers of the colours." (von Suttner 1908, 4)

German Resistance to Hitler and the July 1944 Plot

The cause of peace is a very difficult one to espouse during wartime, especially when the war being waged is against such monstrous evil as Nazi Germany. If any war can be called just, then the war that defeated the vile social, political, and racial injustices of Nazi Germany might perhaps be called one. Although it is unlikely that it alone could have defeated fascist Germany, a secret German resistance movement did exist. The first resistance to Hitler, from about 1933 to 1937, came from the Left, and thousands of German Communists were put into concentration camps. The Nazis treated dissenting Socialists and Liberals in the same brutal way. "Later," writes David Astor, "in about 1937 there began a new kind of intensely secret opposition. It was centred on Army officers, the only class in the community that could possibly overpower the SS. And it was this alliance between Army officers and a range of civilian contacts that made the only coup against Hitler that nearly succeeded in July 1944" (*Times Literary Supplement*, 5 February 1993).[9]

As early as October 1939 there were papers exchanged and meetings arranged between Prince Max von Hohenlohe and the Foreign Office in London concerning a possible basis for peace. But as Colville (then Prime Minister Chamberlain's private secretary, and soon to serve Churchill in the same office) remarks in his diary entry for 25 October 1939, "I am afraid the F.O. [Foreign Office] are rather defeatist about the possibility of procuring peace" (1985, 45). An entry for 29 December 1939, however, reads in part: "There are signs of a renewed peace move. The Vatican and Mussolini are putting their heads together and may enlist the support of Roosevelt . . . Our . . . conversations with German army leaders and Hohenlohe, through Conwell-Evans, are continuing and all hope of engineering an internal coup d'état does not seem to be abandoned. It is said that Hitler and his generals are at loggerheads over an invasion of Holland" (60). Once Churchill became prime minister on 10 May 1940, he was adamant in his demand that the Foreign Office should offer "only absolute silence" to all peace approaches. It was in January 1943 at Casablanca that the Western leaders promulgated their war aims, including the demand for unconditional surrender of Germany, thus destroying any possibility of rapprochement with the German resistance movement.

In the name of the courageous group of conspirators including Count Claus Schenck von Stauffenberg, S.A. General Count Wolf-Heinrich von Helldorf, Hans-Bernd von Haeften, Gottfried von Bismarck-Schönhausen, and officials of the information department of the German Foreign Office in Berlin, Adam von Trott zu Solz had tried over and over again to interest the Allies in getting rid of Hitler and setting up an interim government in Germany, but without success. Realizing that the Allies offered no assistance, Adam von Trott and his friends decided that they must act without outside help. Trott told Christabel Bielenberg, "From now on this is a German affair. We must rid ourselves of this régime by ourselves, and . . . it will be done. It will and must be done, before the Allies have to do it for us" (Bielenberg 1984, 147).

Ultimately this led to the unsuccessful attempt to assassinate Hitler by von Stauffenberg and to the arrest and execution of all those brave and desperate people concerned. Missie Vassiltchikov was also a close friend of Adam von Trott. Her diary has several entries concerning the July 1944 plot and the subsequent trial of the conspirators (Vassiltchikov 1987, 189 et seq.). The 1944 plot is deservedly famous in the historical lists of courageous acts of the Second World War.

The savage executions followed at Plötzensee prison where, in blinding lights and to the whirring of film cameras, each man convicted in the conspiracy against Hitler's life was strung up on a butcher's hook attached to a high beam and strangled not with rope but with piano wire, so that death would come slowly from strangulation rather than from a sudden broken neck. The event belongs on the long list of atrocities that are part of the painful and undeniable historical legacy of the Second World War.

The Allies' unhelpful policy regarding efforts within Germany to negotiate a peace, most commentators suggest, arose because it was very difficult to sort out "good" from "bad" Germans as the war went on with increasing atrocities, suffering, and destruction. In actual fact, German resistance was not a popular movement; it was made up of a number of different and often unrelated activities by various individuals or groups, such as the White Rose resistance group. Oldfield, using the term "Germany's Antigone," recounts the courageous activities of Sophie Scholl and her brother Hans who were members of White Rose. They were students at Munich University, and were decapitated in February 1943 for distributing subversive leaflets. (Oldfield 1989, 132–61; Vassiltchikov 1987, 207). Furthermore, apart from the assurances of people like Adam von Trott, there was every evidence that Hitler acted and spoke for the entire German nation. Nevertheless, the history of the Second World War might have been different, and many lives and cities might have been saved, if the peace initiative within Germany—that "other Germany"—had been taken more seriously not only by the Allies but by the general population of Germany itself. This was the problem for the conspirators against Hitler: there simply weren't enough like-minded Germans to support them. In actual fact, reports that came out after the war show that "the attempted coup was not well received by either the man in the street at home or the military at the front. Even the churches formally condemned it" (ibid., 207)

The End of Women's War Work

The revelation of women's courage is not new in history. What was new in the First World War was the way that courage liberated women from many social restrictions and moral boundaries: in 1919 it seemed they had won freedom and some sexual equality. The same set of circumstances again prevailed in 1939–45. Women were forced to leave their homes and families to work in the best interest of the state, and in so doing enjoyed social if not economic equality; but again, they were directed to return to their homes and families in the best interests of the state in 1945. This, in spite of Churchill's words:

And I am sure of this—that when victory is gained we shall show a temper as admirable as that which we displayed in the days of our mortal danger. In all this the women of Britain have borne, are bearing and will continue to bear a part which excited admiration among our allies, and which will be found to have definitely altered these social sex balances which years of convention have established. (Quoted by Saywell 1985, 1)

Most of these brave and resourceful women on both the home front and in the armed services had little time for reflection on the significance of war and their war work. They were caught up in a dire situation in which it was first necessary to stop Nazi Germany from taking over all of Europe, including Great Britain. But one thing the war had done for many of them was for the first time to make them politically aware. They joined unions, lobbied for equal pay and for day nurseries. But gender influenced attitudes are less susceptible to change than politics and war: these women gave up their war work and returned to their domestic world in vast numbers in 1945. However, they did not forget the relative freedom and independence their war jobs had afforded them; in the 1960s many of these women and their daughters joined in the women's movement. Moreover, thousands of them joined the antinuclear protest groups of the sixties, seventies and eighties, campaigning for total disarmament.

5

British Women and Men Poets
of World War II

"Luck was against you, poet, that you lived when guns
And trampling feet was all that mankind knew of poetry"

In the previous chapters I have tried to suggest some of the historical circumstances that generated the poems I turn to now. In this final chapter, concerned with the poetry of women and some of their male counterparts written during the Second World War, we see, as in chapter 2, how the experiences of war translate into literature, and into poetic form in particular. These real-life experiences are clearly not just incidents in a poetic text; they are representations and responses to the terrifying impact of war on these women and men poets.

My main source for women's poetry written between 1939 and 1945 is *Chaos of the Night*—the companion volume to *Scars Upon my Heart,* hereafter referred to as *Chaos*— edited by Catherine Reilly (1984).

Although it is true to say that most of the attitudes to war and poetry were influenced by World War I, parallels between the two world wars must be made carefully. As in that war, for instance, women and men poets respond to what is happening to themselves and to humanity at large in the terms, symbols, and logic of poetry. Each of them explored the meaning of war, or its meaninglessness, and in so doing tried to convey the truth of war as each of them perceived it. To read them is to feel the burden of their fate. Death, pain, and suffering color all their poetry. On the other hand, despite Wilfred Owen's statement that all a poet could do was warn, most World War II poets do not seem to moralize so much as record as accurately as they can whatever it was that could be felt and expressed. Keith Douglas, the poet nearest to Owen as one whose poetry is centered in battlefield experience, said something very similar, that to be lyrical about war was to be inappropriate.[1]

Both Stephen Spender and Robert Graves believed that the new war poetry would be different from that of World War I. They did not believe that the war would produce another Rupert Brooke or Wilfred Owen (or May Sinclair or Rose Macaulay, they might have added; women writers seem not to enter their minds) because ". . . moods of naif enthusiasm and of spiritual defeatism are equally unsuited to our times. There was an implicit rejection of the 'prophetic role that Owen had given to a poet in times of war, and a general agreement that the term 'war poetry' was misleading because to the extent that it dealt with human suffering, it was simply 'poetry'" (Banerjee 1976, 99).

Yet, according to Brian Gardner, editor of one of the finest war anthologies, *The Terrible Rain* (1978), the three most important poets, Sidney Keyes, Alun Lewis, and Keith Douglas, were all conscious of their First World War predecessors, "particularly Lewis of Edward Thomas and Douglas of Isaac Rosenberg" (xx). Many critics agree that the Great War rooted itself in the imaginative consciousness of Europe as a powerfully mythopoeic historical event.[2]

In *English History 1914-1945*, A. J. P. Taylor concluded that the battle of the Somme, with its massive casualties and blundering generals, had "set the picture by which future generations saw the First World War" (1965, 108). The battle of the Somme was the archetypal image of modern warfare, preposterous in its cruelty, violence, and savage waste of life, and probably more powerful than any other war image until the discovery of the concentration camps and the atomic bombing of Hiroshima and Nagasaki. It was a catastrophic event that did not, mercifully, involve women directly. The negative side of women's historical absence from the battle of the Somme was that they were not, as Claire Tylee points out, part of the mythos of this epic event and therefore not part of its subsequent imaginative representations (1990, 1–17).[3]

Unlike World War I, conscription of men began at the start of World War II. And for the first time in British history there was conscription of women, from December 1941. Many of the men, especially perhaps the poets among them, felt they were a doomed generation, doomed by the failure of the First World War to solve Germany's problems; they just had time to be born and reach call-up age when the war was declared in 1939. They felt condemned by the past and not very hopeful of the future. Perhaps because women were playing a much bigger and newer part in World War II than in 1914–1918, their experience as recruited members of the WAAF, the ATS, and the WRNS absorbed them; it was a first time for women, and it must have had its own excitement and offered a tremendous sense of emancipation and purpose, whereas the men (or their fathers) had witnessed, with massive casualties and irreparable wounds, the face of war, very close up and not long ago.

Everyone honored and mourned those who had died in World War I at least once a year on Armistice Day, 11 November, when a collective act of remembrance was paid to all those who had lost their lives in the Great War. Yet the young servicemen of 1939 had been taught to question the values of their fathers, and to believe that patriotism, loyalty, and obedience were often a disguise for enslaving the individual in the service of the state. Vernon Scannell writes that the mood commonly found everywhere among the armed forces was one of skeptical resolution and resignation, even in 1939 (1976, 19). As Lewis said in a letter to his wife, "Acceptance seems so spiritless, protest so vain. In between the two I live" (Robert Graves's introduction to Lewis's *Ha! Ha! Among the Trumpets, Poems in Transit* 1945, vi).

Of course women, too, suffered cruel losses in the Great War, in spite of the common perception that it was a "men only" war. Many of them had worked very hard to help prevent the 1939 catastrophe and were consequently in an anxious, even alienated state when war was declared. The point is that most of the women in the armed services, who were relatively young, must have felt a certain optimism in their new jobs, albeit an optimism that became more and more qualified as the war went on. Some of their poetry reflects these changing moods. As I have suggested in the previous chapter, however reluctant the women and men of Britain were to go to war, and whatever a "just war" meant to them, they accepted the necessity of defeating Nazi Germany— alone, if everyone else failed. F. Tennyson Jesse puts the position quite clearly in her poem "Note to Isolationists 1940":

> With you there are blue seas, safe seas,
> Ships that go their ways with tranquil breath.
> Here there are black seas, cold seas,
> And ships unlit that go down to death.

You have the snug homes, the safe homes,
Men who are safe in work or play.
Here there are broken homes, burnt homes,
But hearts undefeated to meet each day.

We have the common men, the quiet men,
Who'd not change the perils that they run
For the safe place and the safe men—
Ours in the shadow for yours in the sun.

(*Chaos*, 69)

Anne Ridler historicizes war in her poem "Now as Then," arguing for a just war this time. While the poem reveals that she has few illusions about war in general, or past wars—"War is not simple: in more or less degree / All are guilty . . . / Yet those earlier English, for all their psalms / Were marauders"—still she trusts that the end of the war might herald a new age of cooperation in Europe.

And since of two evils our victory would be the less,
And coming soon, leave some strength for peace,
Hopeful like Minot and the rest, we pray:
'Lord, turn us again, confer on us victory.'

(*Chaos*, 105)

Dorothy Sayers also hoped for a just victory in her poem "The English War":

And send, O God, the English peace—
Some sense, some decency, perhaps
Some justice, too, if we are able,
With no sly jackals round our table,
Cringing for blood-stained scraps.

(H. Gardner 1966, 46)

But when the time came for the women as for the men, it brought the bitterest victory, one which involved the unimaginable catastrophes of the concentration camps and of Hiroshima and Nagasaki. Anne Ridler's "Now" could never be like "Then" again. Those men poets born in the early twenties belonged to a generation "brought up," as Alix Comfort remarked, "in the certainty that it would be killed in action on behalf of an unreality against an insanity" (Hewison 1977, 114). For Comfort, the answer to this sense of alienation and isolation was pacifism.

Hewison reports that forty published poets were killed in the war. Brian Gardner tells us that of the 119 poets in his anthology, *The Terrible Rain*, "almost one in six was silenced in that conflict" (xvii). Three of the four soldier poets generally considered to be the most significant Second World War Poets were killed in action: Sidney Keyes in 1943, Alun Lewis in 1944, and Keith Douglas in 1945; only Roy Fuller, who served in the navy but did not actually see battle, survived. Both Lewis and Douglas tried to unite the disparate parts of their poetic selves—poet and soldier—in action. The man as soldier, they thought, acquired authority on behalf of the man as poet. Lewis also wanted the experience of combat to help him in the long fight for peace. Lewis turned down the offer of an instructor's job in order to remain on active service so as "to share the comradeship of war, and of death" (Fuller 1973, 135).

Although women were still restricted to noncombatant roles, the nature of the war meant that they were extensively exposed to enemy action as both servicewomen and civilians. The writers and poets among them no longer had to rely on incidentals and imaginative identification with the battlefront, as they had in World War I. They were at the scene of battle—frequently under fire—in a military if not combat capacity. It was total war, and the women on the home front had as great an experience of terror, tension, and anxiety of war as the women and men in the armies at the front. The fear of death, injury, and mutilation no doubt helped civilians to understand the same catastrophic fears of their men and women in the battle zones.

How the experience of war transforms itself into literature is a complex question, as is the question of what particular form seems most appropriate, particularly for women. That the mythopoeic quality of war is suited to poetry is well known. I would suggest that the deep emotional and psychological experiences of war, its daily tragic happenings, its fear and its sacrifices, speak directly to women's consciousness, and that for the expression and representation of these experiences women turn naturally to poetry as the form that allows them to say most accurately what it felt like to be a woman in wartime in the 1940s. For many poets the war was less a social-political situation than one of human suffering and death. As well as being the form for forces of emotional experience, poetry also requires techniques of concision which suit well the exigencies of wartime writing. It is far easier to carry around a poem in draft form than, say, a novel or even a short story.

Many women poets of World War II were not professional poets or writers; indeed, most of them were not, unlike the men
included in this chapter, who were mostly writers of one kind
or another—poets, journalists, editors, reviewers, and so on.
Much of the women's writing was an intensely personal response
to the war. Some women were writing for the first time; many of
them stopped writing after the war. In other words, their writing
was of the sort that is unlikely to be written except in wartime.
These women wrote under great emotional stress, and once the
stress was relieved, there was no further need to write. Others,
such as Edith Sitwell and Patricia Ledward and Anne Ridler,
were well known as poets and editors before the war.

Edith Sitwell was a successful poet in the thirties for whom
the war became a main inspiration. She wrote one of the best-
known poems of the war, "Still Falls the Rain," during an air
raid in 1940; yet nonetheless she was included in only one of
the four anthologies of the best World War II poetry (B. Gardner
1966), other than *Chaos*. It seems that the old perception still
persisted that war was a man's business and that only the masculine experience of war was worth selecting and anthologizing.
Yet, as many commentators have acknowledged, women were
subjected to as much danger and injury as men in this war.

In 1942 Patricia Ledward coedited an anthology with Colin
Strang, "Poems Of This War By Younger Poets." Even this anthology reflects a general problem with anthologies of war poetry:
the minor presence in them of women's poetry. Poems by six
women and thirty men appear in it. Taking its title from a line
by Edith Sitwell, "The Terrible Rain," Brian Gardner's anthology
of 1966, generally thought to be one of the best, includes 5
women and 113 men. Selwyn's collection of 1985, whose criteria
for selection were that "the poetry is written by British and Com-
monwealth forces serving in the Second World War, and it was
written *during* that war . . ." (Selwyn 1985, xxiv), has seven
women and 200 men. And this in spite of the editor's remarks:
"Finally, in one undisputed way, the Second World War produced a group of poets hardly known in the First World War:
women poets" (xxiii). "Hardly known" seems a bit of an under-
statement considering that both of Reilly's anthologies exclusively devoted to women's poetry of the two world wars had been
published in 1981 and 1984 respectively.

Scars Upon My Heart contains 125 poems by seventy-nine
women, and *Chaos of the Night* 137 poems by eighty-seven
women. Both books are a by-product, Reilly tells us, of her main

field of interest, the bibliography of the poetry of the two world wars.[4] We have much to be grateful for since these two anthologies alone reclaim poems that might otherwise be lost to us forever, having first appeared in works now long out of print. Being anthologized depended very much on where the poet was first published. And of course anthologies can be advantageous or not to poets: on the one hand there is not the weight of a given body of work, and on the other hand the best poems may be selected, leaving the reader unaware of the weaknesses of the poet's other work.

Many different sorts of poems appear in *Chaos of the Night*, and they vary in skill, but all express genuine and relevant attitudes towards women's experience of the war. The poetry is one way of constructing and transmitting women's history of the war—a history that was written at the time and that we continue to talk about. Women's writing at this time was the result of tensions and terror, passions and pity, anger and grief, boredom, loss, disgust, religious hopes, longings and fears for absent husbands, lovers, and brothers, weariness, anxiety, fears for children and family, and desires for peace.

The men poets of World War II deliberately avoided "poetic" language and rejected the glorification of war and false patriotism. The men wanted their verse to be anchored in the truth of the moment—in battle, on leave, in the mess and barrackroom— in simple concrete language. Of course these poets were aware of their predecessors such as Spender, Graves, MacNeice, and Auden, as well as the ancients and the Neo-Georgians—there was a lot to take on board, what Ted Hughes has called "the terrible, suffocating, maternal octopus of ancient English poetic tradition" (introduction to Keith Douglas's *Selected Poems* 1964, 12).[5]

Most critics agree that the soldier poets of World War II used a plain vocabulary and laconic style. They had to find a language for what the romantic tradition could no longer express, and they did this in simple, ordinary language. Alun Lewis will serve as an example here; I quote from stanza 3 of "Burma Casualty" (To Capt. G. T. Morris, Indian Army):

> "Your leg must go. Okay?" the surgeon said
> "Take it" he said. "I hate the bloody thing."
> Yet he was terrified—not of the knives
> Nor loosing that green leg (he'd often wished
> He'd had a gun to shoot the damned thing off)

But of the darkness that he knew would come
And bid him enter its deep gates alone.

(Lewis 1945, 59)

Did the women write with these constrictions of language and style in mind, or did they write simply to express ideas and intense feelings about the impact of the war upon their lives? Their writing is often more explicit than the men poets, and they use little irony. Were many of them less within the poetry-writing tradition and consequently less conscious of the continuation of a literary form? The contrast here is that although the men were aware of their predecessors, the women as poets had relatively few predecessors since those few they had were grossly underrepresented in the war anthologies and other publications of the interwar years. This represents nothing new in the history of literature, where men have long been central and women marginalized. But we must also consider that many women poets would have thought of themselves as poets, not specifically women poets, and so would not have looked only at women poets as their predecessors.

There are some striking differences between Reilly's two anthologies, and one of them is that there is far less sentimentality in the World War II anthology. Of course sentimentality does not long survive personal experience of war, of which women were getting far more than in World War I; moreover, the zeitgeist was against it. To some extent women had found their voices; they write with assurance, with less generality, and this is no doubt partly due to their social-political experience in the interwar years. As the previous chapters have shown, at this time women did have a voice in Parliament (however muted), and thousands of women worked outside their homes, including the majority of women whose hopes of marriage had been buried with their lost loved ones on the battlefields of France. The image of women and their image of themselves had changed greatly in the twenty-odd years between the two world wars.

The mood of *Chaos of the Night* grows out of seeing where the truth lies in women's experience, or recording things apprehended so as to reveal that truth. As someone said, many people felt they were living inside a newsreel film, and this is reflected in the style of these poems. The women did not necessarily feel they were writing "literature." As in *Scars Upon My Heart*, there is much nature imagery; it is not used, however, to contrast a peaceful, fruitful England with the brutality of the trenches—

the mud, the rain, and the rats,[6]—but to convey the endurance
and sanctity of natural forms and rhythms in spite of man's
mechanized destructiveness. The women could not make this
contrast because they usually had no clear image of where the
men were—there was no static trench warfare.

Frances Bellerby's "War Casualty in April" is a good example:

If Man has forgotten tenderness, yet it remains
With the birds feeding the anxious fluttering young.
If Man has rejected compassion, still there persists
As of old the heart-wrenching droop in missel-thrush song.
And Man dreams not of faithfulness such as the lilac tree
Flaunts undismayed beside the broken home.

The brown-coated bulb lay tombed in the drowsing earth
But never forgot its springtime tryst with Life;
Yet Man keeps no tryst with Life: he obliterates
Memory, and hope; he labours to destroy;
Serves Death; . . .

Man's brutal indifference to life, his inability to be faithful to its
natural rhythms, above all to care for it in all its forms is contrasted with the world of nurturing nature. Yet, in spite of man's
cooperation with deathly war machines, which wrench him from
the natural world of which he is a part, nature receives him in
his final rest:

Yet the mercy of the grass
Warm sweetness breathes into this dying face,
And the tender charity of the gentle rain
Washes away the blood from these death-clouded eyes.

(Chaos, 19)

The poet suggests it is only when he is dead that healing, ele-
mental nature can wash and cleanse man of his terrible mistakes,
nurture him back into innocence and peace. The poem implies
a fusion between man and earth which, as a spiritual response
to death, offers consolation in spite of the atrocities of war. To
some extent the poem expresses the romantic idea of nature as
a lost Eden; yet the sense of mortality and the paradox of simulta-
neously enriching nature while debilitating human nature
strengthens the poem's conclusion.[7]

Marion Coleman, a woman doctor who worked in a camp in
southern Italy between 1944–45 when the allied armies were

liberating Europe, describes the effects of the destructiveness of war as a devastating disease that blights and destroys the landscape and all that dwells upon it: villages, houses, people, crops:

> The houses are broken, wasted,
> fields and trees wounded, killed.
> Crosses crowd where corn grew,
> sprouted from bodies hurriedly buried,
> sown deep and thick in the raked soil.
> Warm air distils
> a scent, not of flowers and young leaves,
> but of putrid decay,
> heavy as magnolia, horribly rotten.

Libraries are another feature of the human landscape and of immense significance to intellectual life; they are also brutally and carelessly destroyed:

> Where light shone, order and praise sang softly,
> years of learning were stored
> like honey gold in the comb,
> now is only bomb-struck desolation.

After using the landscape to image the wanton destructiveness of war, the poet goes on to picture war in the age-old metaphor of a monster strangling all life until not a whisper of it is left:

> Death has leapt upon life,
> and the shriek of the encounter
> echoes on and on through silence
> for ever.
>
> (*Chaos*, 31)

Dorothy Wellesley compares and contrasts eternal nature and vulnerable human nature in "Spring in the Park (London: 1919–1943)":

> The sudden crocuses start up, erupt
> Like flames along the stark uncoloured grass,
> Striped mauves, profounder purples, bright, abrupt,
> Strong copper golds. And as the wounded pass,
> Flayed, broken, bled, the snow-wind and the snow
> Gather and pause and charge the earth again,
> Rush the dark sanctity of drought below
> The cedar tree's long levels, plane on plane . . .

The poem ends with the psychological trauma that war inflicts upon all those involved in whatever capacity, the cruel continuance of trauma in the mind, and the unconscious necessity of displacing its destructive impulses onto the other or others.

> There is a woman who has lost her lover—
> She hunts the spring flowers mutely since he died.
> And there a boy, disfigured, daily told,—
> When the kind friend has winced and looked aside,—
> He lost his face to build 'an Age of Gold'.
>
> (*Chaos*, 124)

In "Milk Boy" Wellesley writes of the indiscriminate nature of war in England in 1942. The poem universalizes the savage fate of the innocent young civilian:

> Early this morning at the break of day,
> A boy of sixteen went out for the milking
> Up on the white farm alone on the hill,
> With a single white candle upheld by his hand,
> Carrying his pail through the air so still.
>
> Then came the Nazi, knowing the white farm there,
> The hour of milking white heifers of morning.
> There lay the red pools, with the milk pools mingling
> O there in the sun—in the red sun arising,
> The white boy, the white candle, the white heifer
> Dying. . . .
>
> (*Chaos*, 124)

Perhaps this poem is somewhat sentimental; however, the suddenness of the boy's death falling from the sky so unexpectedly, the spilling and mingling of life's vital fluids of blood and milk starkly convey the wickedness of warfare. The elegiac tone of the last stanza deepens our grief.

Nature imagery in Alun Lewis's and Keith Douglas's poetry is of a different order from the above, and necessarily so, for Lewis was stationed in India and Douglas in the North African desert. In Lewis's poem "The Mahratta Ghats," the Indian landscape is seen in sharp detail, and the sense of place is powerful:

> The valleys crack and burn, the exhausted plains
> Sink their black teeth into the horny veins
> Straggling the hills' red thighs, the bleating goats

—Dry bents and bitter thistles in their throats—
Thread the loose rocks by immemorial tracks.
Dark peasants drag the sun upon their backs.

The poem suggests the harshness of the land, its unproductive-
ness and the immense physical effort and burden involved before
the peasants can get anything out of it to survive. Lewis concludes by identifying both the long-suffering peasant and the
foreign soldier as victims of social and political oppression:

Who is it climbs the summit of the road?
Only the beggar bumming his dark load.
Who was it cried to see the falling star?
Only the landless soldier lost in war.

And did a thousand years go by in vain?
And does another thousand start again?
(Lewis 1945, 43)

Like Keith Douglas, whom he knew at Oxford just before the
war, Sidney Keyes was also posted to North Africa; like Douglas,
he was killed in action. His religiously symbolic poem "The
Wilderness" has the desert landscape for its setting:

The red rock wilderness
Shall be my dwelling-place.

Where the wind saws at the bluffs
And the pebble falls like thunder
I shall watch the clawed sun
Tear the rocks asunder

.   .   .   .

The rock says "Endure"
The wind says "Pursue".
The sun says "I will suck your bones
And afterwards bury you."
(B. Gardner 1978, 111)

The poem owes something to Eliot's *Waste Land*. The landscape,
the wilderness itself, is the key image; the pitiless desert is the
testing place for self-knowledge in wartime, and of religious
faith.

Unlike World War I, women and men in the services were

posted all over the globe, in Europe, Asia, and the Middle East. Keith Douglas was stationed with a tank regiment in North Africa. He images a very different kind of landscape from Europe or India, somehow a more terrifying one, perhaps because more stark, less familiar, full of menace and imminent death. Douglas believed the battlefield was central to a poet's wartime experience where death was the grim reality, casting away all other concerns and illusions. In his poem "Cairo Jag" we have a detailed description of the corruption and sordidness of the Cairo streets and some of its inhabitants seen through an acutely observant, foreign soldier's eyes:

> But there are the streets dedicated to sleep,
> stenches, and sour smells; the sour cries
> do not disturb their application to slumber
> all day, scattered on the pavement like rags,
> afflicted with fatalism and hashish. The women
> offering their children brown paper breasts
> dry and twisted, elongated like Holbein's bone signature.
> All this dust and ordure, the stained white town
> are something in accord with mundane conventions.

The poem concludes by moving out of these dirty city streets with their suffering inhabitants, out into the desert landscape where a different kind of suffering, rottenness and corruption, has taken over:

> But by a day's travelling you reach a new world,
> the vegetation is of iron.
> Dead tanks and gun barrels split like celery
> the metal brambles without flowers or berries;
> and there are all sorts of manure, you can imagine
> the dead themselves, their boots, clothes and possessions
> clinging to the ground. A man with no head
> has a packet of chocolate and a souvenir of Tripoli.
>
> (Selwyn 1985, 72)

The grim reality of this devastating scene of human vulnerability and annihilation and the shockingly simple use of language with which it is conveyed carry us along as if we too were eyewitnesses. The language is unpretentious, yet pure, concentrated yet amazingly casual. It is as if we were seeing a surreal painting and hearing it described in every day conversational language. The pictorial and linguistic interaction produce a nightmarish sense of terror; the mingling of the extraordinary with the ordinary.[8]

Death was a theme common to women and men poets. It seems fair to say that women treated the subject with anguish, anger, grief, and acceptance; they did not, as the men did, express such deep forebodings of their own imminent death—not even, with a few exceptions, women in the services or in the blitz. There may be many reasons for this difference. No doubt what society expected of women at this time was fearlessness and fortitude; these would have been the desirable norms. And women have always been aware of the ease with which the representation of deep emotions and fears can be classified as overreacting, sentimental, and hysterical. Although women seemed to choose poetry as the form best suited to the expression of their unexpressed thoughts and feelings, the required mood of quiet stoicism may have precluded them from imagining in writing their own deaths. To think of the death of their men and of themselves might have been too demoralizing. Violent death may have hung over them, but women still had to do their war work and look after their families. It is also possible that the avoidance of their own death as a subject for their poems was to some extent a defensive mechanism; perhaps the anxiety involved was unconsciously displaced onto poems about the death of others. Women wrote about the death of loved ones, its dreadful waste and the pitiful suffering of the dying, and the great unfillable deathly gaps left in their own lives when a loved one was killed. Particularly moving are two poems by Vera Bax, who lost two sons—both of whom served in the Royal Air Force:

To Richard, My Son
(Killed in Action, August 17, 1942)

I hide my grief throughout the weary days,
And gather up the threads of life again,
Remembering you ever gave your praise
To those for whom fate's hardest thrust was vain.
Now, when I feel my courage flicker low,
Your spirit comes to breathe it into flame,
Until I lift my head, and smiling go,
Whispering softly your beloved name.
And yet to me it seems but yesterday
You were a child, and full of childish fears:
Then I would run to you and soothe away

The loneliness of night, and dry your tears;
But now you are the comforter, and keep,
From out the shadows, watch, lest I should weep.

To Billy, My Son
(Killed in Action, May 15, 1945)

Now comes, indeed, the end of all delight,
The end of forward-looking on life's way,
The end of all desire to pierce the night
For gleam of hope, the end of all things gay;
The end of any promise Spring might hold,
The end of praying and, O God, the end
Of love that waited to be shared and told;
Now, evermore, shall life with sorrow blend;
That sorrow whose dark shape the months had fought,
And strictly kept in confines of the will;
Had held quiescent while each conscious thought
Searched far horizons where joy lingered still;
But, my beloved, fearless, gallant, true,
Here is fair end of sorrow, now, for you.

(Chaos, 13)

These sonnets must be two of the saddest poems in the entire canon of war poetry. The sequence ends with a third sonnet, "The Fallen," written on V.J. (Victory over Japan) Day, 15 August 1945, in which the grieving mother figure is universalized as a stoic survivor, one who must endure and "Have no self-pity now for loneliness; / Permit no tear, no sad, recalling sigh." For Bax, mothering apparently involves loving acceptance of pain and even gladness at the fate of sons who have died young:

Remembering that age too seldom gives
What youth has dreamed: our hopes are mostly vain
And fortunate indeed is he who lives
Forever young, beyond the reach of pain.

(Chaos, 14)

The poet takes comfort that hers is now "the long battle against defeat, / Be not less steadfast in the fight than they" (*Chaos*, 14). While we sympathize with this devastating, crushing loss, we should at the same time reiterate Helena Swanwick's question: "Must we train young men to such mass-murder and idealize them because they risk so much?" (Swanwick 1935, 501). Here we may also recall again the work of another pacifist woman, the German artist Käthe Kollwitz, who took as her theme the opposition of mothers to war. In her representations of the suffering of innocent children, the grief of parents and widows, the fierce need of mothers to protect their young, she created in lithographs, drawings, and sculpture some of the most powerful of pacifist images.[9]

In her poem, "Missing, Presumed Killed," Pamela Holmes writes of another kind of suffering endured by women:

> There is no cross to mark
> The place he lies,
> And no man shared his dark Gethsemane,
> Or, witnessing that simple sacrifice,
> Brought word to me.
>
> There is no grave for him;
> The mourning heart
> Knows not the destination of its prayer,
> Save that he is anonymous, apart,
> Sleeping out there.
>
> But though strict earth may keep
> Her secret well,
> She cannot claim his immortality;
> Safe from that darkness whence he fell,
> He comes to me.
>
> (Chaos, 61)

The poem speaks for a religious sacrifice and a belief in immortality, a comfort Vera Bax denies herself. The five-line stanzas and the solemn rhythm of the last line of each one organize the mourning experience into a hymnlike pattern of religious faith, and comfort. The idea of a shared sacrifice by patriotic means to a divine end offered the Christian women of both world wars immense comfort. But fewer poems occur on this theme in women's poetry of World War II than in World War I. England was a far more Christian country in the first two decades of this century than in the second two.

Most significantly, some women poets saw in the death of loved ones the death of their unborn daughters and sons. No doubt if the soldier poets who were married had thought of the death of their wives in the war, they, too, might have grieved over never-to-be-born children. I have not discovered men's poems with this theme as their subject, although many men poets write with

longing for the quiet domestic life of home and children they
have been separated from. (Both Sidney Keyes and Keith Douglas
were unmarried.) Sarah Stafford's poem "The Unborn" speaks
of the ancient curse of war and of its aftereffects; for even when
peace shall come again, it will be

> A haunted peace, for we have done a thing
> The ancient gods, in all their wrath, had wept for.
> We have robbed the world of a myriad human faces
> And twice a myriad beauty-making hands.
> For in the bodies of the slain in battle
> And in the dark wombs of the mourning women
> Lie lovely nations, never to be born.

The poem goes on to lament the irreparable loss of the imaginative worlds that might have been our future music, art and literature, and it comes to the stern conclusion that "Not in eternity
can we atone." From the loss of possible creative artists, the poet
moves angrily to another cruel sacrifice war demands of women
and men:

> So, when a man lays down his lusty life
> To save his land, he says with dying breath,
> 'Here, people, since you need it, is my life
> And my son's life, yes, and my son's son's life,
> And my wife's joy, and all our sums of joy
> And God knows what of richness and delight
> That might have flowed from me. . . .'
>
> (Chaos, 119)

This poem may seem to contradict my statement earlier that
in anticipating their own deaths men do not usually think of
the potential future generations, but it must be noted that the
universalized man in this poem is created by a woman. It is she
who imagines how a man might feel about his unborn sons while
knowing the anger and pity she, and by extension, other women
feel about such enormous tragic loss.

Other poets celebrate maternity as an unbeatable force of nature. Valentine Ackland's "7 October, 1940" is a good example:

> One does not have to worry if we die:
> Whoever dies, One does not have to bother
> Because inside Her there is still another
> And, that one wasted too, She yet replies
> 'Nothing can tire out Nature—here's another!'
>
> (Chaos, 1)

There is an admirable defiance in this poem, but at the same time a lamentable sense of birth and death as some sort of conveyer belt and not much more. Ada Jackson's poem is more ironic, as is her title, "Blessed Event":

> In labour when
> the raid began
> she could not run
> as others ran.
> Now here shall be
> no infant's cry,
> no navel string
> to cut and tie,
> she being—by
> a bomb well sped—
> delivered of
> her soul instead.
>
> (Chaos, 64)

The awareness of death must have been, at some level, a part of everyone's consciousness, but for those serving at the battlefronts it must have been a central and terrifying part of their everyday awareness. Many of the men had a fatalistic attitude and saw death in battle as inevitable, absurd, even obscene, seldom heroic. It is not surprising therefore that the subject of death is treated with great diversity by the writers of war poems. Death in battle is the fate of the soldier, and poets like Douglas, Keyes, and Lewis accepted it as their individual destiny, though not necessarily as the end of future generations.

Keith Douglas's poem "Simplify me when I'm Dead" reminds those who are left of the need to be true to the meaning of the dead soldier's life and experience:

> Remember me when I am dead
> and simplify me when I'm dead.
>
> As the processes of earth
> strip off the colour and the skin:
> take the brown hair and blue eye
>
> and leave me simpler than at birth,
> when hairless I came howling in
> as the moon entered the cold sky.

Of my skeleton perhaps,
so stripped, a learned man will say
'He was of such a type and intelligence,' no more.

Thus when in a year collapse
particular memories, you may
deduce, from the long pain I bore

the opinions I held, who was my foe
and what I left, even my appearance
but incidents will be no guide.

Time's wrong-way telescope will show
a minute man ten years hence
and by distance simplified.

Through that lens see if I seem
substance or nothing: of the world
deserving mention or charitable oblivion,
not by momentary spleen
or love into decision hurled,
leisurely arrived at an opinion.

Remember me when I am dead
and simplify me when I'm dead.

(Douglas 1964, 34)

"Speak of me as I am; nothing extenuate," said Othello; and Hamlet implored his only true friend, Horatio: "Absent thee from felicity awhile, / And in this harsh world draw thy breath in pain / To tell my story." Doomed men want the assurance of the truth about themselves to be told once they are gone; the simple truth. "The truth of a man," says Ted Hughes, "is the doomed man in him or his dead body." Keith Douglas, Alun Lewis, and Sidney Keyes, among other war poets, circle this idea time and time again. Voicing the poet's dilemma between loving and killing, creating and destroying, Sidney Keyes writes from North Africa: "Knowing I am no lover, but destroyer / I am content to face the destroying sun." The sense of foreboding is very strong in Douglas' poem "Simplify me when I'm dead"; he does not say "If I die" but "when I'm dead." Perhaps it is, as Rilke believed, that a man carries death within him, as a woman carries her child.

On the whole women did not seem to think like this; but then they were not exposed to the devastating experiences of the battlefield, and its daily assault upon body and mind. And of course the men at the front were used to the grim reality of seeing their comrades killed with terrifying frequency. On the other hand women were exposed to the indiscriminate bombing of the blitz on the many cities such as London, Liverpool, Coventry, and Cardiff. Servicewomen were similarly exposed to aerial bombardment behind the lines and in the military installations in which they served.

Perhaps there were not so many poets among these women, or there would have been more poems on the subject. However, two poems in *Oasis* directly express the fear of being killed. Winifred Boileau, a member of the ATS, served in an antiaircraft regiment in east London during the blitz. Her poem, "Sounds" (1940), is written in the traditional sonnet form, and the regular iambic pentameter lines and rhyme scheme suggest a closed form of experience from which there is no escape. In addition the frequent use of the *s* sound effectively represents the fearful crackling, hissing, and whistling noises of bombs dropping, windows shattering, and shrapnel exploding. To read the sonnet is to feel acute anxiety and distress.

> The Heinkels drone their dismal nightly dirge,
> The guns spit forth their salvoes, sharp and harsh,
> And whistling bombs and dull explosions merge
> With thunderous land mines, out across the Marsh.
>
> The clanging tocsin of the fire brigade
> Rings in your ears. Through weary hours you lie
> And listen, trying not to be afraid,
> Yet fearing most to be afraid to die.
>
> (Selwyn 1985, 142–43)

The second poem, also in *Oasis*, is by Grace Griffiths, who served in the ATS in Signals. She calls her 1944 poem "Doodlebugs", a slang name for the V1 flying bombs:

> A bomb, last night, fell close by Radlett.
> The pulsing engine stopped right overhead.
> Four minutes to the crash. Slowly we counted;
> One girl cried 'Oh God! Dear God!'
> The tension grew to bursting point; the blast
> Shattered the windows. We breathed again.
> Always the bombs come over in early evening
> Just before we go on shift. We talk of rush-hour traffic

But underneath the fear remains. Death can come
From so many angles. Tomorrow, next week, next month
It may not pass us by.

(Selwyn 1985, 158)

Cecilia Jones, a nurse in Queen Alexandra's Imperial Military
Nursing Service (QAIMNS), served on hospital ships in Italy,
Sicily, Greece, North Africa, and India. Her poem, "Shipbound,"
describes the acute pain and discomfort of the wounded on
board one of these floating hospitals during rough weather:

By day, the ship rolls and the sea is gray.
All things are lashed with rope, for fear they break.
The sky lurches, the sea heaves.
Many are sick and lie down,
Wishing for death, to be still again.
The sea mocks and rolls the ship,
Dashing us from side to side.
The wind howls and flings spray high;
We shut the portholes for fear of wet.
The air is thick, our heads red.

(Selwyn 1985, 273)

Mostly, if women anticipated their own deaths at all, and especially as a result of enemy attack on the military installations
they served, or during bombing raids on the home front, they
addressed themselves to the effect it would have on the living.
Nothing radical or new here: women are often more relationally
oriented than most men; perhaps this is true even when they are
thinking about their own deaths. In any case women much more
frequently anticipated the death of their lovers and husbands in
battle, as in this poem "Immensity" by Mabel Esther Allan:

You go at night into immensity,

. . . .
                    my heart never sings
Now on spring mornings, for you fly at nightfall
From this earth I know
Toward the clear stars, and over all
Those dark seas and waiting towns you go;
And when you come to me
There are fearful dreams in your eyes,
And remoteness. Oh, God! I see
How far away you are,
Who may so soon meet death beneath an alien star.

(Chaos, 3)

First occurs that sense of alienation from the loved one whose dreadful wartime activities remove him from the normal world of family life and feeling. The subtext of the poem is the horrific discrepancy between loving and killing which some of the soldier poets write about, as we shall see later in the chapter. The poem also expresses what must have been one of women's most powerful fears: the fear of having no dear one left. This metaphorical death the women writers do allow themselves to express.

In the *Chaos* collection there is more of a focus on children than there is in the *Scars* poems; although this could be expected in poems written after Hiroshima and Nagasaki, the poems I am focusing on in the second anthology were all written before August 1945. Children were among the most innocent and pitiful victims of the war. Their fathers went away to fight, sometimes never to return, sometimes never having seen them. Pamela Holmes speaks for all those women left to bring up a child who will never know her/his father. In "War Baby":

> He has not even seen you, he
> Who gave you your mortality;
> And you, so small, how can you guess
> His courage or his loveliness?
>
> Yet in my quiet mind I pray
> He passed you on the darkling way—
> His death, your birth, so much the same—
> And holding you, breathed once your name.
>
> (*Chaos*, 62)

Many children were evacuated and so separated from their families and homes; those who remained at home in the cities were subject to the nightly terror of the bombing raids, and toward the end of the war the V1 flying bomb and V2 rocket attacks. Some of these children lost their lives or were badly injured; others saw relatives—some elderly—badly mutilated, buildings destroyed, and people buried alive. At the end of the war many of these children were fatherless and, less frequently, motherless. The traumatic experience of World War II affected many children and caused psychological and social problems that remained unresolved in their subsequent adult lives. In addition to the suffering of the children in their own war-ravaged countries, there was the immense misery and suffering of refugee children.

It goes without saying that in the list of miseries endured by children during wartime, the most horrifying of childrens' fate was that suffered by those in Nazi concentration camps. Let Karen Gershon speak for their disastrous destiny, first in her poem "Home":

> The people have got used to her
> they have watched her children grow
> and behave as if she were
> one of them—how can they know
> that every time she leaves her home
> she is terrified of them
> that as a German Jew she sees
> them as potential enemies
>
> Because she knows what has been done
> to children who were like her own
> she cannot think their future safe
> her parents must have felt at home
> where none cared what became of them
> and as a child she must have played
> with people who in later life
> would have killed her had she stayed.
>
> (Chaos, 47)

Here the conspicuous lack of punctuation symbolizes the lack of any certainty or security in their lives, and the consequent anxiety.

Karen Gershon's second poem, "A Jew's Calendar," speaks of the continuing trauma in her adult life—the guilt of the survivor, passed on by her wartime experience. The significance of the date gives the final stanza its title, "Spring 1945":

> I climbed some stairs to a bare room
> in which the Red Cross lists were spread
> naming the German Jews not dead
> I could not find my parents' names
> so glad was I they could not claim
> compensation from me for
> the martyrdom they had to bear
> that I did not grieve for them.
>
> (Chaos, 48)

The openness of the poem, its lack of any punctuation, suggests a never to be healed wound; one perhaps to hide in; yet the word "martyrdom" implies some consolation for the grieving daughter. After their torment, her parents, she hopes, share the sanctity and serenity of the saints.

There are some women poets who view children in wartime not only as victims but also as creators of moral problems of a particular kind. Sylvia Townsend Warner's complex poem, "Road 1940," about the mothering responsibilities that all women bear to all children begins:

> Why do I carry, she said,
> This child that is no child of mine?
> Through the heat of the day it did nothing but fidget and whine,
> Now it snuffles under the dew and the cold star-shine,
> And lies across my heart heavy as lead,
> Heavy as the dead.

She is not sure why she had saved the defenseless child—abandoned, she supposes, by its own indifferent mother, thrown down in a wheel rut: "Yes, and the woman who left it there has sped / With a lighter tread." The poem moves on to serious moral questions, which the poem does not answer. As a boy-child is its fate to grow up to the horror of killing in more wars, or to starvation? Behind the questions is a painful awareness of the tenuousness of achieving a peaceful, productive life for the extremely vulnerable, unprotected young, and the perils of growing up in a political-social system that has seen two disastrous wars that have claimed the lives of two successive generations. Beyond these considerations the poem asks if human nature is inherently wicked—not only the mother who has abused her child by cruelly abandoning him, but the child itself:

> Though I should save it, she said,
> What have I saved for the world's use?
> If it grow to hero it will die or let loose
> Death, or to hireling, nature already is too profuse
> Of such, who hope and are disinherited,
> Plough, and are not fed.

(Chaos, 123)

The tone of despair matches the grimness of the poet's vision of European society in the 1940s: the culmination of the agonized suffering and misery the political-social situation of the

twenties and thirties had created for many human beings. Some
writers at this time, women among them, had become extremely
demoralized by the effects of communist and fascist policies;
the individual had become enslaved to the all-powerful state.
Although the poet has no illusions about her motivation in helping the child, the poem ends with a symbolically grim resolution,
emphasized by the rhyme scheme, recognizing with muted hope
those in the world who still value, even cherish, children and
those who mother them, especially in disastrous circumstances:

> But since I've carried it, she said,
> So far I might as well carry it still.
> If we ever should come to kindness someone will
> Pity me perhaps as the mother of a child so ill,
> Grant me even to lie down on a bed;
> Give me at least bread
>
> (Chaos, 123)

In "For the War-Children" Sylvia Read concludes with a memo-
rable half line, "And for them must the world be woman" (Chaos,
103). This could also have served as a fitting epilogue to Warner's
poem. The activity of mothering is of vital importance to all of
humanity, and it cannot be sacrificed; but perhaps, as I have
suggested earlier, the concept can be extended as the pacifist
Maude Royden intended, so that the private life-centered experience of ordinary women can be adapted to save the life of the
world.

The previous chapter described in some detail the German air
assault on Britain which began in June 1940. Since most of the
men were called up at the beginning of the war, it was up to the
women and older men to organize themselves and their families
to withstand the nightly bombing. Women played many vital
roles, and their experience is reflected in some of the poetry in
Chaos of the Night. Lois Clark worked as an ambulance driver
for the Civil Defence, driving a stretcher-party car during the
blitz on London. There was always plenty to do since these brave
people were often the first to arrive on the scene after a bomb
attack and were nearly always, as she tells us, "first out:"

> I remember waking,
> from a sort of sleep,
> khaki-clad and rigid on the canvas bed,
> gas mask already slung
> like an obscene shoulder-bag;
> torch in one hand, tin hat in the other,
> . . . .

Pull the starter, oh God make her go!
She goes. Across the yard,
double declutch at the gate, and out—
roaring down the now invisible road
masked sidelights only—roaring down to disaster;
where the bomb-ploughed houses wait
with their harvest of casualties

(*Chaos*, 26)

We cannot claim that this is great, even very good poetry, but it is verse that gives us a picture of the times and speaks for what must have been the experience of many brave women all over bombed-out London. In another poem Clark describes one of the pathetic casualties she must have seen on one of her journeys: an old woman "sitting there / in her big armchair, grotesque under an open sky, / framed by the jagged lines of her broken house" (*Chaos*, 27).

In "Sky-Conscious" Alice Coats writes about the fearful new significances of the sky, so long regarded as harmless, even sheltering, but now full of menace and portents of violent death and destruction, "potencies whereby we live or die." There was a common saying that the moon was no longer a "lovers' moon," but a bomber's moon. In the poem, the night sky is 'Frescoed with searchlights, shells and flares and stars," and "lit with false dawn of fires, and all the bright / Ferocious constellations of our wars." The poem ends on a note of catastrophic doom, greater than anything ever known before: "Jove's superseded thunderbolts at rest, / Aurora and Apollo dispossessed" (*Chaos*, 29).

The enormous destructive power of the high explosive bombs that devastated the city and terrified its inhabitants seems the incarnation of evil to Ethel Mannin in her ironically titled poem, shaped like the body and tail-fins of a bomb, "Song of the Bomber":

I am purely evil;
Hear the thrum
Of my evil engine;
Evilly I come

The stars are thick as flowers
In the meadows of July;
A fine night for murder
Winging through the sky.

> Bombs shall be the bounty
> Of the lovely night;
> Death the desecration
> Of the fields of light.

I am purely evil,
Come to destroy
Beauty and goodness,
Tenderness and joy.

(Chaos, 85)

Edith Sitwell sees evil raining down hideous death and destruction in religious terms. Her powerful poem, "Still Falls the Rain" with the sub-title "The Raids 1940. Night and Dawn," begins:

> Still falls the Rain—
> Dark as the world of man, black as our loss—
> Blind as the nineteen hundred and forty nails
> Upon the Cross.

The poet suggests that ever since Christ died to redeem humanity, we have ignored his redemptive power, nailing him each year since then to the Cross of suffering by our wars and hatreds, atrocities, and brutalities. Yet:

He bears in His Heart all wounds—those of the light that died,
The last faint spark
In the self-murdered heart, the wounds of the sad
uncomprehending dark . . .

And so there is hope in spite of our interminable suicides:

Still falls the Rain—
Then—O Ile leape up to my God: who pulles me doune—
See, see where Christ's blood streames in the firmament:
It flows from the Brow we nailed upon the tree
Deep to the dying, to the thirsting heart
That holds the fires of the world,—dark-smirched with pain
As Caesar's laurel crown.

(Chaos, 114–15)

If the war symbolizes human tragedy, suffering and death, then Sitwell's poem asserts through Christ a kind of tragic affirmation. In spite of the evil and guilt of war, which is the responsibility of all humanity, hope persists, symbolized by the merciful Christ on the Cross: "Still do I love, still shed my innocent light, my Blood, for thee." The hoped-for fusion of the finite with the infinite gives the poem its powerful religious symbolism and meaning.

The necessary correlative to these images of the blitz on London is the poetic image of what it was like for the inhabitants of Berlin to suffer the same fate, although in fact the bombing of Berlin was much more intensive and much more devastating as "Threnody for Berlin—1945," a poem by Wrenne Jarman, puts into perspective the appalling destruction of this great city, the center of the cultural and artistic life of prewar Germany as well as of the vile and transitory Nazi regime:

> Was there no mute to mourn this crumpled city,
> No funeral drape, no stern bell left to toll?
> Does it pass unattended, without pity,
> No requiem said for its delinquent soul?
>
> There where the wind plays through the broken copings
> And toppled keystones mark the death of streets,
> Her veins lie open to the vulture's droppings:
> The blood coagulates, and no heart beats.
>
> Go barehead, even her slaves, in this quenched hour—
> No Sodom raked to ash five thousand years
> Is deader than this mortuum of power,
> Watched, in its final rigor, without tears.
>
> (*Chaos*, 68)

Keith Douglas is also able to identify with the other side—the enemy—in all his similarities, as simply another human being in his poem "Elegy for an 88 Gunner" (also published under the title "Vergissmeinicht" [Forget me not]). The poem is set in the North African desert in 1943. Three weeks after an attack the poet returns to the battlefield and finds—"sprawling in the sun"—a dead soldier who had struck Douglas's tank with a shell from his antitank gun. Lying on the sand is "a picture of his girl / who has written: *Steffi, Vergissmeinicht* / in a copybook Gothic script."[10] The poet moves closer to the dead young man, who might so easily have been himself:

> We see him almost with content,
> abased, and seeming to have paid,

mocked by his durable equipment
that's hard and good when he's decayed.

But she would weep to see to-day
how on his skin the swart flies move;
the dust upon the paper eye
and the burst stomach like a cave.

For here the lover and killer are mingled
who had one body and one heart;
And Death, who had the soldier singled
has done the lover mortal hurt.

(Selwyn 1985, 71)

The poem owes something to Owen's "Strange Meeting." The dilemma the poem ends with is one that haunted many of the soldier poets and that is expressed in a variety of ways: the conflict between loving and killing. The same man can both value the importance of human love, and yet be a killer of other human beings. It is almost as if war compels all those involved to put good and evil behind them. As Douglas says in "How to Kill," another poem on this subject, "How easy it is to make a ghost." Nancy Price's ironic poem, echoing a popular song of the period, makes the same point and the same implicit criticism:

Johnny, take a gun—take a gun—take a gun,
Killing's to be done—to be done—to be done,
Never want to run—want to run—want to run,
Finish with your fun—with your fun—with your fun.

Handle steel—love the feel—death you'll deal,
Pity, mercy crush.
Remember they are mush.
Thousands dead,
Keep your head.

(Chaos, 101)

Frances Cornford's short poem, "Casualties," addresses itself to this painful dilemma of the prewar compassionate person, protective and loving, now engaged in destructive acts of war:

This once protected flesh the War-God uses
Like any gadget of a great machine—
This flesh once pitied where a gnat had been,
And kissed with passion on invisible bruises.

(Chaos, 34)

The question of the moral implications of fighting a war exist alongside what most of those involved accepted as the historical necessity of the mortal struggle. Most women writers shared this view, but at the same time agonized over the right of the state to send their men out to kill. Patricia Ledward's poem in memory of a young friend and poet, Timothy Corsellis, killed flying, expresses this thinking and feeling very clearly:

> You wished to be a lark, and, as the lark, mount singing
> To the highest peak of solitude your soul had found,
> You wished to fly between the stars and let your song
> Shower down to earth in gleaming falls of sound.

But the aspiration of a fighter pilot and poet cannot soar in innocence like the lark, that traditional symbol of poetry; there is historical reality to shoot the whole lovely, tragic idea down:

> World chaos coiled about you, and each upward flight
> Meant struggling with the deep morass of history:
> Luck was against you, poet, that you lived when guns
> And trampling feet was all that mankind knew of poetry.
> . . . .
> A letter tells us you are dead—at twenty years.
> From shocked and nerveless hands the paper slips.
> We see it all—the failing engine, the numb fingers clutching,
> The instantaneous fear, distorted lips.

The identification with the lost loved one is immediate and tragic. The tone is one of despair which turns into one of fevered remembrance; those left behind will "Drink till your memory ferments within our brain." Despair turns into a terrible lament and angry outrage at the senseless waste of life:

> Play on, O Harlem band, O swing your blues!
> Rend every stone with your terrible, lamenting cry:
> Those who would sing of life, and hope, and joy,
> Are driven out to hunt, to kill, to die.
>
> (Ledward 1942, 43-44)

And, incredibly, it has all happened before. The poet Wrenne Jarman compares the two world wars: the same hopes, fears, dreams, and nightmares; same courage; same tragic waste expressed in the refrain *sweet youth goes out to die* of the poem "It Happened Before":

After, came an army back,
Soul-weary and sore,
Through the streets and up the hill
Whence they came before.
But ghosts are marching in their ranks who should not linger
        there—

.   .   .   .

        But the flags are flying bravely and the mourners are not
            nigh.
        Heigh-ho! sweet youth went out to die.

The vision fades. . . . But hark, a bugle
Sounding in the square!
Strong young life is cheap again—
Khaki masses there!

.   .   .   .

        Dry your tears, you silly girl, it does no good to cry.
        Heigh-ho! sweet youth grows tall to die!

                                                    (*Chaos,* 66)

The lighthearted tone of detached despair belies a deep sense
of betrayal and of the incredible, outrageous folly of war and the
enormous human sacrifices involved. Yet, as with the women
poets in World War I, the poets of World War II are deeply aware
of the debt they owe the men who have fought so bravely; there
is even a sense of guilt that others have died for or instead of
them. The question then becomes one of atonement: "Only my
life would be fair sacrifice," says Juliette de Bairacli-Levy (*Chaos,*
8), while Rachel Bates acknowledges her infinite debt to the
"stranger who died for me," asking how shall she "requite his
wounds, his death, who dies unknown / And keeps my feeble
flame alight / With ransom of his own?" (*Chaos,* 11). Some feminists will say that they do not want this sort of sacrifice to be
made on their behalf, but in the Second World War, if we accept
the problematic "just war" idea, where women were not actually
engaged in combat, there could be no alternative. As I have already suggested—indeed it is the argument of this book—one
answer might be for women and men to unite and work not only
nationally but internationally in every conceivable way, especially politically, parentally, and socially to create the political
will and psychological awareness that utterly refuses to consent
to war as a means of solving international conflict. The respon-

sibility for creating peace and preventing war requires everyone's whole hearted participation.

The war had been going on for nearly six years when on 7 May 1945 Germany surrendered. On 14 August 1945, after the atomic bombing of Hiroshima and Nagasaki on 6 and 9 August, Japan surrendered. The atom bomb was the final unimaginable horror in a war full of grotesque horrors. The last six months of the war piled horror on horror, almost blotting out what had preceded it.

I shall end with two poems by women that speak most succinctly to these final obscenities of a disastrous, cruel war. First, an extract from Elizabeth Wyse's haunting poem, "Auschwitz":

> What big heavy doors!
> Strange, lingering odour,
> Faint but still here . . . strong disinfectant.
> 'Stand round the shower point'.
> Wait for water. Don't think about the crowd.
> They don't notice your degradation.
> They can't see your shaved head from all the rest!
>
> . . . .
>
> Gas! Gas! Gas! Panic!
> The screams, the clutching,
> Pulling, scrambling.
> The total terror of realisation.

(*Chaos*, 129)

And a poem by Margaret Wainwright that speaks to generations of women and the burden they bear as women in wartime:

> O Susanna, Susanna, don't you cry—
> It's 1917 and you'll
> Have a husband by and by.
> He's coming from the Messines Ridge,
> Susanna, don't you cry.
>
> O Susanna, Susanna, don't you cry—
> It's 1933 and you
> Have children who rely
> On what you can scrape up for them
> From a dole that's running dry.
>
> O Susanna, now, Susanna, don't you cry,
> Your son is just on twenty, and

It's time for him to die
In a blazing fighter-bomber like
A comet down the sky.

O Susanna, now, Susanna, don't you cry,
With seven little grandchildren
All growing up so high:
In peacetime with the atom bomb,
Susanna, don't you cry.

(*Chaos*, 122)

These poems represent twentieth-century barbarism: total war. Many of them attempt to address the profound moral problems posed by this most terrible of human activities. Pity is the key word, what Owen famously called the "untold truth" of war: "The pity of war, the pity war distilled." Compassion—pity—is surely one of the profoundest of human feelings and one that this war poetry teaches us to value highly. It teaches us to recognize the essential connectedness of all human beings—to see that for one to kill another is a crime against them all.

Warfare is one form of human behavior, possibly its most aberrant form in its appalling release of violent aggression and destructiveness. Wars will only cease when this form of behavior becomes outdated, when something else is invented to take its place. That something else one hopes might be international humanism in which women and men unite and work together to create a political will and a psychological mentality that will reject war as the last resort in times of international conflict.

Conclusion

The questions of contemporary feminists regarding the connections between women and war, the gender alignment of issues such as the protected and the protector, and war as a distinctly masculine creation, all go back at least to the women's experience of World War I. It seems fair to say that these issues were not given top priority by the women who actually worked for the war effort of 1914–18 and 1940–45, both on the home front and behind the. battle lines. These problems were mostly first articulated by women writers, often pacifists of the times, and by women writers and academics during the following decades, and especially after the Vietnam War, the Falklands War, and more recently, the Gulf War. My study seeks not only to place this ongoing debate (now stretching out to such war-shattered societies as Northern Ireland, Somalia, and Bosnia) primarily in its literary setting of the two world wars, but also to show how literature articulates the historical-social reality of war. By contrasting the voices of men and women war poets, by examining the reasons for the different and at times wavering stands women took on war and peace, and by chronicling the various degrees of resistance or collusion that one finds at times of war I hope to offer the reader a new perspective on this tragic period in European history and on the enormous ethical dilemma war presents.

The period 1914–45 was a time of immense political and social change for women in Britain and in Germany. The suffragist movement, begun in 1851 in Britain and in 1865 in Germany, gained irresistible force during World War I, and by the end of the war in 1918 women in both countries had gained the vote. As we have seen, the wartime achievements of women in Britain and Germany helped create the right climate of opinion for this important legislation, which the women themselves insisted they needed so as to play their part in the reconstruction of their respective societies, both devastated by four years of war. But during the twenty years between World War I and World War II, although women were enfranchised, they still did not achieve much political power either in Britain or in Germany. The right to vote did not automatically gain these women rights in other spheres. For example, British women were not admitted to the ranks of the Foreign Office between the wars, and they were consistently under-represented in the British Parliament and in the Reichstag. Of course after the Nazis came to power in March 1933, no woman could be elected to any political position in the Reichstag.

Between the wars political women in Britain tended to concentrate on improving women's rights to divorce, abortion, and property, efforts that left them little time and energy for the difficult task of campaigning for parliamentary seats. Social justice and professional interests attracted women's services more than the struggle to acquire political equality with men. No doubt women thought and hoped discrimination against them would disappear after World War I; it did not. This unjustified optimism was a mistake for in September 1939 it resulted in a situation not much better than that which had prevailed in Britain at the beginning of World War I. Before women were enfranchised they were a minority that had little voice in foreign policy and in decisions about going to war. What international women should have done in the twenty years between the two world wars was to solidify their political power so that they could vitally affect the policies of their countries. If women's political freedom and justice were to prevail, many more women were needed in parliaments than were present in the interwar years.

In Britain the difficulties that women faced in being selected to constituencies put the odds very much against women politicians. But very gradually women were being educated politically and learning how to participate in electoral processes and parliamentary life. Nevertheless, it is worth remembering that of the nine women parliamentarians in 1939, none was in the cabinet. The total number of women who sat in Parliament between 1919 and 1945 was thirty-eight: seventeen Conservative, sixteen Labour, four Liberal and one Independent.

It is one of the arguments of this book that the under-representation of international women in political life and in positions of power contributed to the climate of opinion that resulted in two devastating world wars that killed millions. Moreover, women themselves, although emancipated, did not work hard enough to promote a peace-loving mentality that would foster negotiation and reject murderous violence as a means of solving international conflict. Generation after generation of fathers, husbands, sons, brothers and lovers went to war, and generation after generation of women and men in Britain and Germany, France, and America allowed this to happen because they did not organize themselves sufficiently against the blandishments of nationalism and militarism.

Both wars had a profound effect upon women, transforming their image of themselves in radical and irreversible ways. The two world wars provided women with important opportunities to work outside the home, as munition workers, land-army workers, policewomen, doctors, nurses, and ambulance drivers, and eventually in 1941 as conscripted servicewomen. Women's courage is not new in history. In spite of the apparent liberation of women from some social and moral restrictions, and the gain of a degree of sexual equality as a result of World War I, in the Second World War they were again required to take up war work, with a consequent transient approach to social and sexual— though not economic—parity; but they reverted to domestic life after the war as a result of social circumstances and government policy. Gender, it seems, is even less open to change than politics and war. Yet the psychological, social, and economic impact of World War II succeeded in sowing the seeds of the future women's movement of the nineteen sixties and seventies and the eventual advance to almost full economic and social status with men.

But this book is not so much about the historical-social period of the two world wars as it is about the literature of these wars and the interweaving of the connections—the similarities and the differences—between the works of the two eras. In particular, I have been concerned with the poetry that articulates the perspectives on the historical, social and cultural realities of these tragic years in Europe in the first half of the twentieth century. For it is above all in reading the poetry of these two wars that as women and men we come to understand and respond to the horror of war as the most terrifying of human activities.

The mood of the poetry of both world wars by women and men reflects a search for the truth in the experiences of war and of relating the human cost of war. To read this poetry is to feel the burden of fate placed upon these women and men who were also poets, addressing—in most of their poems—the profound moral problems of human destructiveness and its terrifying consequences.

The subject of war, of horrific death and senseless destruction, is conveyed to us in a poetic language that grew out of a tradition of heroic verse into the biting satire of Ida Bedford and Siegfried Sassoon, the pitying imagery of Rose Macaulay and Wilfred Owen, of Edith Sitwell and Charlotte Mew. This poetic language of World War I is mostly avoided by the poets of World War II such as Patricia Ledward, Sylvia Townsend Warner, Keith Douglas, and Alun Lewis, in a search for an almost casual plainness with which to convey the devastating impact of war on human life and lives. These poets, whose fathers had fought in the war to end all wars only twenty years before, now believed that if war was to be perceived as the most barbaric of human activities it must not be glamorized and glorified in the language of poetry. How would Homer have written about the battle of the Somme, the destruction of Dresden, and the unimaginable catastrophes of Hiroshima and Nagasaki? That civilization can only build on sympathy and justice for all, and that war and civilization are utterly incompatible are the twin burdens of much of this war literature.

Most of the women and men poets of both world wars were, whether intentionally or not, writing peace literature. To respond to the spectrum of their reactions to war is to understand the essential barbarism involved in sending generation after generation to the killing grounds of war. The poetry is a desperate and moving record of the gross folly of war, an implicit warning that to kill one person is to wound every other person.

Poets, women and men, are not politicians or historians; they are not legislators of the world; but the women and men poets of World War I and World War II together have spoken as if with one voice against the monstrous evil of war, its essential barbarism and the incalculable damage it does to human life. All poets can do is warn; it is up to the rest of us to heed them.

Notes

Chapter 1. Women's Experience of World War I

1. See Roger Fulford, 1957, *Votes for Women*; Hannah Mitchell, 1968, *The Hard Way*; Jane Lewis, 1984, *Women in England: 1870–1950*; Dale Spender, 1982, *Women of Ideas and What Men Have Done With Them*.

2. See Braybon and Summerfield, 1987, *Out of the Cage* for a comprehensive account of working women in both world wars.

3. See Elizabeth Sarah's biographical essay in Spender 1983, 278–80.

4. Harrison sums up Emmeline Pankhurst's extraordinary and contradictory view as follows: "Fortunately for woman suffrage, she lay low for the next few months" (209).

5. See various accounts of this stormy and momentous meeting in Strachey 1928, 351; Oakley 1983, 196; and recently Wiltsher 1985, 71–72.

6 According to Partridge, the etymology of the phrase "to show the white feather" goes back to 1842, and was standard English by 1895. "A cross-bred game-cock has a white feather in the tail" (*A Dictionary of Slang and Unconventional English*, [London: Routledge & Kegan Paul, 5th ed. 1961], vol. 1, 269)

7. Vellacott's paper drew upon the 1965 publication, *Pioneers for Peace*, the history of the Women's International League for Peace and Freedom, (1915–1965) compiled by Gertrude Bussey and Margaret Tims. Vellacott reexamined the history of how women got the vote.

8. Helena Swanwick, The Kingsway Hall meeting of 13 May 1915, during which women were given a report of the Women's International Peace Congress at The Hague, 28 April to 1 May 1915. Reported in *Towards Permanent Peace*, Fawcett Library Periodicals Archive, Guildhall University, London.

9. Sewall's 1915 *Women, World War and Permanent Peace* is a record of the International Conference of Women Workers to Promote Permanent Peace, chaired by Sewall in San Francisco, 4–7 July 1915. It describes the founding of the Women's Peace Party by Jane Addams in January 1915, as well as the early organization of the International Women's Conference at The Hague. See especially 95–107.

10. Record of the International Women's Congress at The Hague, 28 April–1 May 1915. At this congress there were present: from Austria, six; from Belgium, three (officially sent; there were five later); from Canada, two; from Denmark, six; from Germany, twenty-eight; from Great Britain, three (about one hundred eighty were prevented from attending by the cancellation of the boat service between England and Holland); Hungary, nine; Italy, one; U.S., forty-seven; Brazil, one; Ottoman Empire, one; Australia, one; Holland, one thousand (Fawcett Library Holdings, London: Guildhall University). See also Swanwick 1972, *Women and War*.

11. According to some sources, the German embassy issued a warning to passengers written in general terms, which was printed in the New York morn-

ing papers on 1 May 1915, directly under the notice of the sailing of the Lusitania. In her autobiography Lady Rhondda gives an eyewitness account of the shipwreck from which she and her father escaped. She mentions that in New York there was "much gossip of submarines" during the weeks preceding the last voyage of the Lusitania. It was freely stated and generally believed that a special effort was to be made to sink the great Cunarder so as to inspire the world with terror (Rhondda 1935, 240–58).

12. See Anne Wiltsher's 1985 comprehensive study of women pacifists of World War I: *Most Dangerous Women*. She states that all women might have been prevented from voting if pacifism had been really influential.

13. Moorehead writes that in spite of their harrowing experiences during the war at the hands of the tribunals and the army, these men felt they had won some sort of victory for their belief. There was a feeling that "they had seriously challengéd the state's supremacy over the individual. Never again, many of these sixteen thousand men would say, was it going to be possible for a man's moral stand to be ignored, nor for a democracy like Britain to take such a harsh line towards its dissenters. The war protesters had not yielded; that was the point, and the British public, having witnessed their endurance, were now prepared to understand and even respect their position" (79–80).

14. Elshtain's study covers the ancient Greeks to the present. See also *Images of Women in War*, eds. Sharon Macdonald, Pat Holden, and Shirley Ardener, 1987, for a history of women's relation to war, violence, and revolution since the French Revolution.

15. The total number of British soldiers killed in World War I was approximately 908,371; those seriously injured numbered 2,090,212, and the number of prisoners of war reported was 191,652. (War Office Statistics, 1922). The total number of Allies killed (excluding the British figure) numbered approximately 4,314,300; the total number of the Central Powers killed, 3,412,000. The total Allied and Central Powers' killed numbered roughly 8,634,000 (T. C. Charman 1975, 45).

16. See also: Morgan 1975, 149–50; Rover 1967, 205; Fulford 1957, 108.

Chapter 2. British Women Poets and Soldier Poets of World War I

1. In 1978 Catherine Reilly published *English Poetry of the First World War: A Bibliography* in which she identified 2,225 British men and women—civilians, and servicemen—who had written verse about the Great War. "Of these 2,225 at least 532 were women and at least 417 (men and women) served in the armed forces or other uniformed organisations such as the Red Cross, the Special Constabulary, and the Voluntary Aid Detachment." See Reilly's introduction to *Scars Upon My Heart* (1981), xxxiii–iv. The anthology is the result of her curiosity as to why the 532 women whose writing about World War I she had discovered in book, pamphlet, and broadsheet form had "faded into oblivion."

2. Some of these recent anthologies include *The Penguin Book of First World War Poetry*, ed. Jon Silkin (London: Penguin, 1979); *Up The Line to Death: The War Poets 1914–1918*, ed. Brian Gardner (London: Methuen, 1964); Jon Stallworthy, *Poets of the First World War* (Oxford: Oxford University Press, 1974).

3. See Margaret Randolph Higonnet et al., editors of *Behind the Lines: Gender and the Two World Wars* (New Haven and London: Yale University Press, 1987); Sandra M. Gilbert and Susan Gubar, *No Man's Land* vol. 2 (New Haven, and London: Yale University Press, 1989); Jean Bethke Elshtain, *Women and War* (New York: Basic Books, 1987); Betty A. Reardon, *Sexism and the War System* (New York: Teacher's College Press, 1985); Claire M. Tylee, *The Great War and Women's Consciousness* (Iowa City: University of Iowa Press, 1990); see also Hinz, *Mosaic* 23.3 (1990): 151–73.

4. Sandra Gilbert, "Soldier's Heart: Literary Men, Literary Women, and the Great War," in *Signs* 8.3 (1983): 446.

5. This is an objection several commentators have raised to Gilbert's article "Soldier's Heart." See Jane Marcus, "The Asylums of Antaeus: Women, War, and Madness: Is There a Feminist Fetishism?" in *The Difference Within: Feminism and Critical Theory* (1988), 50–81; Claire M. Tylee, "Maleness Run Riot— The Great War and Women's Resistance to Militarism," in *Women's Studies International Forum* 11.3 (1988): 199–210, where she states that Gilbert "ranges indiscriminately between American and British experience, between women of different generations, and between different social groups." See also D. M. Hooley's critique, "Art and Catastrophe," in *Times Literary Supplement* (London), 1–7 September 1989, 945.

6. See Freud 1920, "Thoughts in Time of War," *Standard Edition of the Complete Psychological Works*, vol. 22 (London: Hogarth Press, 1964). See also Moorjani's chapter on the fragmented body motif in *The Aesthetics of Loss and Lessness*, 45–61.

7. As Eric Leed points out, this identification was psychically dangerous since "Each departure could be compensated for only by an intensification of the bonds to those who remained, and this guaranteed that the next, inevitable loss would mean an even more severe, even less tolerable extinction of the self." *No Man's Land: Combat and Identity in World War I* (Cambridge: Cambridge University Press, 1979), 210.

8. For example, a friend is a comrade, a horse is a steed, the enemy is the foe, danger is peril, to conquer is to vanquish, to attack is to assail, to be earnestly brave is to be gallant, the dead on the battlefield are the fallen, to die is to perish, the front is the field, to win is to conquer, one's death is one's fate, what is contemptible is base, and so on. (Fussell 1975, 21–22).

9. In fact we could say that the war poets created a new style of writing compared with their immediate forebears, for example the Georgians. Many critics besides Fussell have discussed this matter; see for example Mildred Davidson, *The Poetry Is in the Pity* (London: Chatto & Windus, 1972); Roy Fuller, *Professors and Gods* (London: Andre Deutsch, 1973); Vernon Scannell, *Not Without Glory* (London: Woburn Press, 1976); A. Banerjee, *Spirit Above Wars* (London: Macmillan, 1976). Both Owen and Rupert Brooke wrote in the Georgian style before the war. Brooke, who was killed in the Dardanelles in 1915, hardly had time to change his style.

10. It is interesting that Rose Macaulay evidently had a "front-line" experience and, in this particular poem, writes as violently as the men do.

11. Kate Courtney is one of several famous pacifist women Oldfield writes about in *Women Against the Iron Fist* (1989). Courtney, Oldfield suggests, offers us a model of war resistance that could be quite crucially relevant to the late twentieth century. "Kate Courtney's rejection of the very concept of an 'enemy' even in the midst of a mass-murdering war, as well as during the crucial years

when enmity, unscrutinized, built up to that war, holds a vital lesson against acquiescence in our own Cold War" (45). The Cold War may be a thing of the past, but still savage wars rage throughout the world.

12. Speaking of Vera Brittain's nursing experience, Claire Tylee suggests that "the self-image of the Pietá permitted vicarious physical contact with a helpless, 'safe' lover, who was Saint/Knight/Christ, and it made acceptable, even desirable the fact that Roland [Vera's fiancé who was actually killed in the war] would have to be wounded first" (*The Great War and Women's Consciousness* [1990], 73). It took Brittain—and many other women who, like her, suffered tragic personal losses— several years to see through this deadly idealism which sanctioned and sanctified the hideous murderousness of World War I. Poets like Owen and Sassoon saw it in action and so saw through it at the time.

13. Mildred Davidson (1972) suggests that "the simple and sincere lyric carrying the expression of the individual man is characteristic of twentieth-century war poetry" (*The Poetry is in the Pity*, 19).

14. See Angela Moorjani's (1992) chapter on Käthe Kollwitz: "Of Kollwitz's anti-war statements, it is then perhaps her statues of the bereft parents, the mother with the artist's face, the father with Karl's, in grieving postures side by side in the cemetery in Flanders, that most effectively contest the deadly conceptions of sacrifice" (*The Aesthetics Of Loss and Lessness*, 122).

15. "The soldiers broke open the door with the butt-ends of their rifles, and rushed into the ward. At a sign from the police officer . . . the corporal seized Miss Cavell roughly. He tore out of her hand the lint with which she was about to bind the wounded man, and began to drag her away. The Englishwoman, astonished but calm and dignified, asked for an explanation. The answer was a cuff" (Hill, *The Martyrdom of Nurse Cavell*, 1915, 25–26).

16. See Introduction to *Scars* xxv.

17. Owen: "Here is a gas poem, done yesterday, . . . The famous Latin tag means of course It is sweet and meet to die for one's country. Sweet! and decorous!" (Letter 552, 16 October 1917, in Owen, Collected Letters, 499)

18. According to the O.E.D. *sap* (v.t.) is the making of trenches.

Chapter 3. Women between the World Wars, 1918–1939

1. See Roger Fulford, *Votes for Women* (London: Faber & Faber, 1957), especially, chapter 2, and Hannah Mitchell, *The Hard Way* (London: Faber & Faber, 1968); David Mitchell, *Monstrous Regiment* (New York: Macmillan, 1965); David Morgan, *Suffragists and Liberals* (Oxford: Blackwell, 1975); and Constance Rover, *Women's Suffrage and Party Politics in Britain, 1866–1914* (London: Routledge & Kegan Paul, 1967).

2. See Harrison, *Separate Spheres* (New York: Holmes & Meier, 1978), chapter 3.

3. See Vallance's 1979 account of the early history of women parliamentarians in *Women in the House*, 5–43. See also Brookes, *Women At Westminster*, 1967, especially "Heirs and Warming Pans," 3–52.

4. Quoted in Cynthia White, *Women's Magazines 1693–1968* (London: Michael Joseph, 1970), 99, and in Braybon and Summerfield, *Out of the Cage* (London: Pandora Press, 1987), 222.

5. Gail Braybon, 224. See in general, her chapter "The Position of Women Workers in the Twenties," in *Women Workers in the First World War*, 1981,

216–32. See also Jane Lewis, *Women in England 1870–1950*, 1984, particularly her chapter on women in the 1920s.

6. As early as 1907 Finland had granted women the vote; Norway did the same in 1913, Denmark and Iceland in 1915, and Holland in 1917. The Russian revolution also gave women the vote in 1917. Britain, Germany, Hungary, and Sweden all gave the vote to women in 1918.

7. See Jill Stephenson, *Women in Nazi Society*, 1975; Ruth-Ellen Joeres and Mary Jo Maynes, *German Women in the Eighteenth and Nineteenth Centuries*, 1986. See also Richard J. Evans, *The Feminist Movement in Germany 1894–1933*, 1976.

8. Luxemburg had been devastated by the sellout of the "strongest socialist party in Europe" when in August 1914 the Reichstag delegation of the Social Democratic Party of Germany cast its 110 votes in support of the government's request for war credits. Luxemburg spent the war years in and out of prison and was murdered in 1919. In the twenties and early thirties her comrades consistently denounced the capitalist leaders for whom workers' lives were cheap; they were "the cheapest most expendable commodity of all, especially the proletariat."

9. By the middle 1920s women's representation in the Reichstag actually dropped to about six percent, although it rose to nine percent in the 1932 election. See Stephenson 1975, 16; Pore 1981, 51; Rupp 1978, 12; and Evans 1976, 274–5.

10. Speaking of the French socialist women's movement, Joeres and Maynes make a useful distinction between "Socialists who saw capitalism as the cause of women's oppression but argued that it oppressed some women more, or even rather, than others, and nationalist feminists who believed that women were systematically oppressed because of their sex" (1986, 53).

11. See J. C. Fest, *The Face of the Third Reich*, 1970, 129; see also Ramona M. Rose, *Position and Treatment of Women in Nazi Germany*, 1984, 19–25 and Kirkpatrick, *Nazi Germany: Its Women And Family Life*, 1938, 126–48.

12. In Britain in the twenties and thirties this policy of the Labour Party was partly to keep women out of the powerful unions.

13. I am of course aware that the Nazis were not simply interested in increasing the number of childbearing women, but also just as bent upon excluding many women from bearing and raising children—and men from begetting them—through the process of sterilization. However, the important and complex subject of the Nazi's theory and practice of "scientific racism" is beyond the scope of my present study. See Kirkpatrick 1938, 174–203; Bock, 1983, 400–421, and Eickhoff 1986, 44.

14. Most commentators are severely critical of Scholtz-Klink, regarding her as thoroughly evil. Evans 1976, refers to her "ruthless energy" (256). Kirkpatrick, writing in 1938, concludes his chapter on the Führerin: "As participants in the Nazi experiment, German women were prepared to listen to the Nazi verdict as to woman's place" (99). For an extensive account of Scholtz-Klink, see Koonz, *Mothers in the Fatherland* (1987).

15. See Butler's 1986 account of these young women in *Hitler's Young Tigers*. He tells the story of Hildegard Trutz, who gave birth to a *Lebensborn* child and then returned to marry her long-standing SS fiancé (85–87).

16. For example, in *Male Fantasies* Theweleit writes that it is important to remember that in Germany the reality of mass murder, pronatalism, forced abortions, and sterilizations and the whole ugly pattern of legalized racism

depended upon the Nazi fantasy of the survival of the separate sphere of feminine, familial, and maternal realm as a sacred place to be defended at all costs (1987, vol. 1). In other words, in this context the ideological association of the separate sphere with women and peace and the preservation of life is highly questionable.

17. See Koonz's (1987) chapter "Courage and Choice", 309–44 especially 336–38 where she refers to 'Lilo' Hermann's execution and also gives Hanna Elling's list of women who died for their resistance to Nazi rule.

18. After Pearl Harbor was attacked and the U.S. declared war on Japan and Germany, Emily Balch of American WILPF counseled members "not to obstruct the war but to work against hatred and for world co-operation" (Bussey and Tims, 173). Evidently at this moment Balch was not an absolute pacifist.

Chapter 4. Women's Experience of World War II

1. There is something to be said for the argument that Hitler was a direct product of the infamous Versailles Treaty of 1919 that so impoverished Germany in its demands for reparations. This argument proposes that Hitler did not create Nazi Germany, but that the state created him.

2. Gertrude Bussey and Margaret Tims' fine history of WILPF, *Pioneers for Peace*, gives a detailed account of the organization from its inception in 1915 to 1965, and I am much indebted to this source for many of my facts about WILPF.

3. Sybil Oldfield's book is helpful in general for its focus on international women pacifists of both world wars: *Women Against the Iron Fist*, 1989.

4. According to Fitzgibbon, "The British Special Operations Executive (S.O.E.) functioned in a twilight zone between direct military activity, political activity in the German-occupied countries in assisting some of the resistance movements, and sabotage or commando-type operations usually but not always against 'intelligence' targets. Their processing of captured enemy documents and the interrogation of enemy prisoners further blurred the distinctions among various forms of intelligence and para-intelligence activity" (1978, 325–26). See also M. R. D. Foot, *SOE in France*, 1966.

5. See Cynthia Enloe, *Does Khaki Become You?*, in which she examines the ingredients and implications of the ideology of militarism for women. "The military as an institution and militarism as an ideology are distinct phenomena" (9). But today there are other feminists who argue for equality of women in the military and strongly support women being allowed in combat in U.S. forces. Levin et al. in "Feminist Teaching in a Military Setting: Co-optation or Subversion?" explore feminist teaching in the military and its effect on the system. These writers see women's "traditional alignment with pacficism and their daily struggles with discrimination as the obstacles which currently hinder them from making great strides in the military," *Women's Studies Quarterly*, 12:2 (1984): 13–15.

6. Braybon and Summerfield summarize women's experience of both world wars: "Although there were many changes, there was an undertow pulling women back during both world wars, by emphasising that change was temporary, that women were 'really' wives and mothers, and their place was at home, and that they were doing skilled, important jobs and earning relatively high wages on sufferance" (*Out of the Cage*, 1987, 281). The transitoriness of the

change in women's social roles has much to do with women's political failure to consciously develop themselves as a cohesive group.

7. See Denise Riley's 1987 assessment of the position of postwar British women: "Far from war work serving to revolutionize women's employment on any serious level, it was characterized as an exceptional and valiant effort from which women would thankfully sink away in peacetime. This characterization was heavily underscored by pronatalism" ("Some Peculiarities of Social Policy concerning Women in Wartime and Postwar Britain," in *Behind the Lines, Gender and the Two World Wars,* 261).

8. The historical response to the brutality of Harris' mass bombing campaign was evident in letters to *The Times* on the occasion of the erection of a statue of him outside St. Clement Danes church in London on 30 May 1992. The statue was commissioned by the Bomber Command Association (*The Times* 26, 29 May 1992).

9. See various recent correspondence in the *Times Literary Supplement* on the character of German resistance to Hitler: von Hassell, Lamb, 27 November 1992, Evans, Robinson, 11 December 1992, and Astor, 5 February 1993. See also Patricia Meehan, *The Unnecessary War,* 1991.

Chapter 5. British Women and Men Poets of World War II

1. In his essay "English Poetry Of The Two World Wars" Roy Fuller argues against the view expressed by John H. Johnston in *English Poetry of the First World War,* that the poets in that war were "hampered in the expression and evaluation of their experience by their reliance on the lyric . . ." (*Professors and Gods,* 120).

2. See Paul Fussell, 1975, *The Great War and Modern Memory;* Bernard Bergonzi, 1965, *Heroes' Twilight: A Study of the Literature of the Great War;* John H. Johnston, 1964, *English Poetry of the First World War;* and Vernon Scannell, 1976, *Not Without Glory.* Hewison writes of the search for a unifying myth, one that would be the source of values for the individual, that went on during World War Two. He quotes John Lehmann, the editor of *Penguin New Writing,* trying to explain the sense of isolation he noticed in his contributors:

> "It is from the absence of a generally accepted myth or system of beliefs that it arises; a myth whose wholeness would heal the wound between war and peace-time occupation, between the past and the present, between one class and another; a myth which we in England felt we were about to recapture for one moment of astonishing intensity in 1940, when everything seemed to be falling into place." (*Under Siege,* 1977, 180)

3. Tylee's recent book, *The Great War and Women's Consciousness,* 1990, addresses the problem of discovering the cultural significance of women's writing of World War I. She asks the question, "does there exist an imaginative memory of the First World War which is distinctly women's?" (15).

4. See also Catherine Reilly, 1978, *English Poetry of the First World War: A Bibliography.*

5. Feminists might debate Ted Hughes' use of the word "maternal" here, but the sea in poetry has always been symbolically female. I'm not so sure about octopuses.

6. It is also true that the battlefields of World War II were much more

various than in World War I, and women at home would not have had a consistently real image of them. In letters home men were not allowed to say where they were except in the most general terms.

7. Although my frame of reference in this chapter is women and men poets of World War II, it is interesting to compare Bellarby's poem with the third stanza of a famous World War I poem by Isaac Rosenberg, "Dead Man's Dump," in the *Penguin Book of First World War Poetry*, ed. Jon Silkin, 1979, 211:

> Earth has waited for them,
> All the time of their growth
> Fretting for their decay:
> Now she has them at last!
> In the strength of their strength
> Suspended—stopped and held.

8. Discussing Marie Douglas' selection of her son's poems, Ted Hughes writes in his 1964 introduction: "To begin with, perhaps he takes Auden's language over pretty whole, but he empties it of its intellectual concerns, turns it into the practical experience of life . . ."; and later he says, "There is nothing studied about this new language. Its air of improvisation is a vital part of its purity. It has the trenchancy of an inspired jotting, yet leaves no doubt about the completeness and subtlety of his impressions, or the thoroughness of his artistic conscience" (Hughes, *Selected Poems of Keith Douglas*, 12–13).

9. See Note 14, Chapter 2. (Moorjani 1992, *The Aesthetics of Loss and Lessness*, 122)

10. This poem has been printed in a number of versions under at least three titles. I have used the version from Selwyn's 1985 Oasis Selection as it is claimed that Douglas revised this just before his death in Normandy in 1944. In *Keith Douglas, Complete Poems*, ed. Desmond Graham, 1978, an interesting variant on p.140 titled "The Lover" has a footnote that reproduces the entire message written on the photograph:

> Mein Mund ist stumm, aber mein Aug'es spricht
> Und was es sage ist kurtz—Vergissmeinnicht.
>
> > Steffi

(My mouth is mute, but my eyes speak / And what is said is brief—forget me not.)

Here *vergissmeinnicht* is spelled correctly.

Works Cited

Akhmatova, Anna. "July 1914." In *First World War Poetry*, ed. Jon Silkin. Harmondsworth: Penguin, 1979.

Astor, David. *Times Literary Supplement*. London: 5 Feb. 1993.

Ayers, Pat. *Women at War*. Birkenhead: Liver Press, 1988.

Banerjee, A. *Spirit Above Wars*. London: Macmillan Press, 1976.

Bebel, August. *Women Under Socialism*. New York: New York Labor News Press, 1904.

Bergonzi, Bernard. *Heroes' Twilight: A Study of the Literature of the Great War*. London: Constable, 1965.

Berry, Paul, and Alan Bishop, eds. *Testament of a Generation: The Journalism of Vera Brittain and Winifred Holtby*. London: Virago, 1985.

Bielenberg, Christabel. *The Past Is Myself*. London: Corgi Books, 1984.

Blunden, Edmund. *Poems 1914–1930*. New York and London: Harper & Brothers, 1931.

———, ed. *The Poems of Wilfred Owen*. New York: Viking Press, 1931.

Bock, Helen. *Racism and Sexism in Nazi Germany: Motherhood, Compulsory Sterilization and the State, Signs* 8:3 (1983): 400–421.

Braybon, Gail. *Women Workers in the First World War, the British Experience*. Totowa, N.J.: Barnes and Noble Books, 1981.

Braybon, Gail, and Penny Summerfield. *Out of the Cage: Women's Experiences in Two World Wars*. London and New York: Pandora Press, 1987.

Brittain, Vera. *Lady into Woman*. London: Andrew Dakers, 1953.

———. *Letters to Peace-Lovers*. Fawcett Library Archives Guildhall University: London.

———. *Seed of Chaos*. London: New Vision Publishing Co., 1944.

———. *Testament of Youth*. London: Virago, 1978.

Brookes, Pamela. *Women at Westminster*. London: Peter Davies, 1967.

Bussey, Gertrude, and Margaret Tims. *Pioneers for Peace, Women's International League for Peace and Freedom 1915–1965*. 1965. Revised Edition, London: George Allen and Unwin, 1980.

Butler, Rupert. *Hitler's Young Tigers*. London: Arrow Books, 1986.

Cambridge Women's Peace Collective. *My Country Is the Whole World*. London: Pandora Press, 1984.

Charman, T. C. *Modern European History Notes 1789–1945*. Croydon, England: Telles Langdon Publications, 1975.

Churchill, Winston. *The Grand Alliance*. 1950. New York: Bantam, 1962.

———. *Their Finest Hour*. 1949. New York: Bantam, 1962.

Collier, Richard. *1940: The World in Flames.* Harmondsworth: Penguin Books, 1980.

Colville, John. *The Fringes of Power.* London: Hodder and Stoughton, 1985.

Costello, John. *Love, Sex, and War: Changing Values 1939–45.* London: Collins, 1985.

Davidson, Mildred. *The Poetry Is in the Pity.* London: Chatto & Windus, 1972.

Dobell, Mrs C. Oliver. *Son of Mine.* Printed privately, 1915. Available Fawcett Library Archives, Guildhall University, London.

Douglas, Keith. *Complete Poems,* ed. Desmond Graham. London: Oxford University Press, 1978.

———. *Selected Poems,* ed. Ted Hughes. London: Faber & Faber, 1964.

Eickhoff, F. W. "Identification and Its Vicissitudes in the Context of the Nazi Phenomenon." *International Journal of Psychoanalysis* 67 (1986): 33–44.

Elshtain, Jean Bethke. *Women and War.* New York: Basic Books, 1987.

Enloe, Cynthia. *Does Khaki Become You?* London: Pluto Press, 1983.

Evans, Richard J. *The Feminist Movement in Germany 1894–1933.* London and Beverly Hills, Calif.: Sage Publications, 1976.

Evans, Richard J. *Times Literary Supplement.* London: 11 Dec. 1992.

Fawcett Library Archives. Guildhall University London.

Fest, Joachim C. *The Face of the Third Reich: Portraits of the Nazi Leadership.* Tr. Michael Bullock. New York: Pantheon Books, 1970.

Fitzgibbon, Constantine. *Secret Intelligence in the 20th Century.* London: Panther Books, 1978.

Foot, M. R. D. *SOE in France.* H.M. Stationery Office, 1966.

Freud, Sigmund. *Standard Edition of The Complete Psychological Works.* Vol. 22. London: Hogarth Press, 1964.

Fulford, Roger. *Votes for Women.* London: Faber and Faber, 1957.

Fuller, Roy. *Professors and Gods.* London: Andre Deutsch, 1973.

Fussell, Paul. *The Great War and Modern Memory.* New York: Oxford University Press, 1975.

———. *Wartime.* Oxford: Oxford University Press, 1989.

Gardner, Brian, ed. *The Terrible Rain.* London: Methuen, 1966. Reprint, 1978.

———. *Up the Line to Death: the War Poets 1914–1918.* London: Methuen, 1964.

Gardner, Helen, ed. *The New Oxford Book of English Verse 1250–1950.* Oxford: Oxford University Press, 1972.

Gellhorn, Martha. *The Face of War.* London: Virago, 1986.

Gilbert, Sandra M. "Soldier's Heart: Literary Men, Literary Women, and the Great War." *Signs* 8:3 (1983): 422–51.

Gilbert, Sandra M., and Susan Gubar. *No Man's Land.* Vols. 1 and 2. New Haven and London: Yale University Press, 1989.

Graves, Robert. *Good-bye to All That.* New York: Doubleday Anchor Books, 1957.

———. Introduction to *Ha! Ha! Among the Trumpets* by Alun Lewis. London: Allen and Unwin, 1945.

Harrison, Brian. *Separate Spheres.* New York: Holmes and Meier, 1978.

Hassell, Fey von. *Times Literary Supplement*. London: Nov. 27, 1992.

Hewison, Robert. *Under Siege, Literary Life in London 1939–45*. New York: Oxford University Press, 1977.

Hibberd, Dominic, ed. *Wilfred Owen: War Poems and Others*, London: Chatto & Windus, 1973.

Higgins, Ian, ed. *The Second World War in Literature*. Reprinted with additional text and corrections from *Forum For Modern Language Studies 21: 1*. Edinburgh: Scottish Academic Press, 1986.

Higonnet, Margaret R., Jane Jenson, Sonya Michel, and Margaret Collins Weitz, eds. *Behind the Lines: Gender and the Two World Wars*. New Haven: Yale University Press, 1987.

Hill, W. T. *The Martyrdom of Nurse Cavell*. New York: Dutton, 1917.

Hinz, Evelyn, ed. *Troops and Tropes: War and Literature. Mosaic* 23:3 (1990).

Hobhouse, Emily. In Sewall, *Women, World War and Permanent Peace*. San Francisco: John Newbegin, 1915.

Hughes, Ted. Introduction to *Selected Poems* of Keith Douglas. London: Faber & Faber, 1964.

International Women's News 35, no. 2 (November–December 1940). British Library Periodical Holdings, Colindale, London.

Irons, Evelyn. *London Evening News*, Sept. 15, 1939.

Joeres, Ruth-Ellen B., and Mary Jo Maynes. *German Women in the Eighteenth and Nineteenth Centuries*. Bloomington: Indiana University Press, 1986.

Johnston, John H. *English Poetry of the First World War*. Princeton, N.J.: Princeton University Press, 1964.

Kahn, Nosheen. *Women's Poetry of the First World War*. Lexington: The University Press of Kentucky, 1988.

Kazantzis, Judith. Preface to *Scars Upon My Heart: Women's Poetry and Verse of the First World War*. London: Virago, 1981.

Key, Ellen. *War, Peace and the Future*. Tr. Hildegard Norberg. Reprint, New York: Garland Publications Inc., 1972.

Kirkpatrick, Clifford. *Nazi Germany: Its Women and Family Life*. Indianapolis and New York: Bobbs-Merrill Co., 1938.

Koonz, Claudia. *Mothers in the Fatherland*. New York: St. Martin's Press, 1987.

Lamb, Richard. *Times Literary Supplement*. London: 27 Nov. 1992.

Ledward, Patricia, and Colin Strang, eds. *Poems of This War by Younger Poets*. Introduction by Edmund Blunden. Cambridge: Cambridge University Press, 1942.

Leed, Eric J. *No Man's Land: Combat and Identity in World War I*. Cambridge: Cambridge University Press, 1979.

Lewis, Jane. *Women in England 1870–1950*. Bloomington: Indiana University Press, 1984.

Liddington, Jill. *The Long Road to Greenham*. London: Virago, 1989.

Macdonald, Sharon, Pat Holden, and Shirley Ardener, eds. *Images of Women in War*. London: Macmillan, 1987.

Marcus, Jane. "The Asylums of Antaeus: Women, War, and Madness: Is There a Feminist Fetishism?" In *The Difference Within: Feminism and Critical*

Theory. Ed. Elizabeth Meese and Alice Parker. Philadelphia: Benjamins, 1988. 50–81.

Marks, Elise. "The Alienation of 'I': Christa Wolf and Militarism." In *Troops versus Tropes: War and Literature,* ed. Evelyn Hinz. *Mosaic* 23:3 (1990): 73–87.

Mead, Margaret. *Blackberry Winter, My Early Years.* New York: Morrow, 1972. Quoted in *My Country Is the Whole World.* Cambridge Women's Peace Collective, 1984.

Meehan, Patricia. *The Unnecessary War. Whitehall and the German Resistance to Hitler.* London: Sinclair-Stevenson, 1993.

Minns, Raynes. *Bombers and Mash.* London: Virago, 1980.

Mitchell, David. *Monstrous Regiment.* New York: Macmillan, 1965.

Mitchell, Hannah. *The Hard Way.* London: Faber & Faber, 1968.

Moorehead, Caroline. *Troublesome People: The Warriors of Pacifism.* Bethesda, Md.: Adler & Adler, 1987.

Moorjani, Angela. *The Aesthetics of Loss and Lessness.* New York: St. Martin's Press, 1992.

Morgan, David. *Suffragists and Liberals.* Oxford: Basil Blackwell, 1975.

Newberry, Jo Vellacott. "Anti-War Suffragists." In *History* 62 (1977): 411–25.

Oakley, Anne. *Feminist Theorists.* New York: Random House, 1983.

Oldfield, Sybil. *Women Against the Iron Fist.* Oxford: Basil Blackwell, 1989.

Owen, Wilfred. *Collected Letters,* eds. Howard Owen and John Bell. Oxford: Oxford University Press, 1967.

———. *The Collected Poems,* ed. C. Day Lewis. London: Chatto & Windus, 1963.

———. *The Poems,* ed. Edmund Blunden. New York: Viking Press, 1931.

———. *The Poems of Wilfred Owen,* ed. Jon Stallworthy. London: Hogarth Press, 1985.

———. *War Poems and Others,* ed. Dominic Hibberd. London: Chatto & Windus, 1973.

Pankhurst, Emmeline. *My Own Story.* New York: Hearst's International Library, 1914.

Pankhurst, E. Sylvia. *The Life of Emmeline Pankhurst.* New York: Houghton & Mifflin, 1937.

———. *The Suffragette Movement.* London: Longmans, Green & Co., 1931.

Partridge, Eric. *A Dictionary of Slang and Unconventional English,* Vol. 1 269. 5th edn. 1961, London: Routledge & Kegan Paul.

Pore, Renata. *Conflict of Interest: Women in German Social Democracy, 1914–1933.* Westport, Conn.: Greenwood Press, 1981.

Raeburn, Antonia. *The Militant Suffragettes.* London: New English Library, 1974.

Ramelson, Maria. *Petticoat Rebellion.* London: Lawrence & Wishart, 1967.

Rathbone, Eleanor. *War Can Be Averted,* London: Victor Gollancz Ltd., 1938.

Reardon, Betty A. *Sexism and the War System.* New York: Teacher's College Press, 1985.

Reilly, Catherine. *English Poetry of the Second World War: A Bibliography.* Boston: G. K. Hall, 1986.

———. *English Poetry of the First World War: A Bibliography.* London: Prior, 1978.

———, ed. *Chaos of the Night: Women's Poetry and Verse of the Second World War.* London: Virago, 1984.

———. *Scars Upon My Heart: Women's Poetry and Verse of the First World War.* London: Virago, 1981.

Rempel, Gerhard. *Hitler's Children: The Hitler Youth and the SS.* Chapel Hill and London: University of North Carolina Press, 1989.

Rhondda, Lady Margaret. *This Was My World.* London: Macmillan, 1935.

Riley, Denise. "Some Peculiarities of Social Policy Concerning Women in Wartime and Postwar Britain." In *Behind the Lines. Gender and the Two World Wars,* by Higonnet et al. New Haven: Yale University Press, 1987.

Robinson, C. Derek. *Times Literary Supplement.* London: 11 Dec. 1992.

Rose, Ramona M. *The Position and Treatment of Women in Nazi Germany.* Vancouver, B.C.: Tantalus Research, 1984.

Rover, Constance. *Women's Suffrage and Party Politics in Britain 1866–1914.* London: Routledge & Kegan Paul, 1967.

Rupp, Leila. *Mobilizing Women for War: German and American Propaganda, 1939–1945.* Princeton, N.J.: Princeton University Press, 1978.

Sarah, Elizabeth. *Christabel Pankhurst: Reclaiming Her Power.* In *Feminist Theorists,* ed. Dale Spender. New York: Pantheon Books (Random House), 1983.

Sassoon, Siegfried. *Counterattack and Other Poems.* New York: Dutton, 1918.

———. *Diaries,* ed. Rupert Hart-Davis. London: Hart-Davis, 1983.

———. *Selected Poems.* London: William Heinemann Ltd., 1925.

———. *The War Poems,* ed. Rupert Hart-Davis. London: Hart-Davis, 1983.

Sayers, Dorothy. "The English War." In *The Terrible Rain,* ed. Brian Gardner. London: Methuen, 1966. Reprinted 1978.

Saywell, Shelley. *Women in War.* Toronto: Penguin Books. 1985.

Scannell, Vernon. *Not Without Glory: Poets of the Second World War.* London: Woburn Press, 1976.

Schreiner, Olive. *Woman and Labour.* 1911. Reprint. London: Virago, 1978.

Selwyn, Victor, ed. *Poems of the Second World War, the Oasis Selection.* London: Everyman's Library and The Salamander Oasis Trust, 1985.

Sewall, May Wright. ed. *Women, World War and Permanent Peace.* San Francisco: John Newbegin, 1915.

Sharp, Evelyn. "The Congress and the Press." In *Towards Permanent Peace.* (1915) London: Fawcett Library Archives, Guildhall University, London.

Sheepshanks, Mary, ed. *Jus Suffragii—The International Woman Suffrage Alliance Newspaper,* Geneva and ed. *Pax International—The Newsletter of the Women's International League for Peace and Freedom* (WILPF). Geneva.

Sheridan, Dorothy, ed. *Wartime Women: A Mass-Observation Anthology.* London: Mandarin Paperbacks, 1991.

Silkin, Jon. ed. *The Penguin Book of First World War Poetry.* London: Penguin Books, 1979.

Sitwell, Edith. *Collected Poems of Edith Sitwell.* London: Duckworth, 1930.

Sorley, Charles Hamilton. *Marlborough and Other Poems*. Cambridge: Cambridge University Press, 1916.

Spender, Dale. *Women of Ideas and What Men Have Done With Them*. London: Routledge & Kegan Paul, 1982.

Spender, Dale, ed. *Feminist Theories*. New York: Random House, 1983.

Stafford, Jean, ed. *Woman's Newspaper*. British Library Periodical Holdings, Colindale, London 1939.

Stallworthy, Jon. *Poets of the First World War*, Oxford: Oxford University Press, 1974.

Stephenson, Jill. *Women in Nazi Society*. New York: Barnes and Noble, 1975.

Strachey, Ray. *The Cause*. London: G. Bell & Sons, 1928.

von Suttner, Bertha. *Lay Down Your Arms; the Autobiography of Martha von Tilling*. Tr. T. Holmes. London: Longmans Green & Company, 1908. First published as *Die Waffen Nieder*, 1885.

Swanwick, Helena. *I Have Been Young*. London: Gollancz, 1935.

———. Report on the Kingsway Hall Meeting of 13 May 1915. In *Towards Permanent Peace*. (1915) London: Fawcett Library Archives, Guildhall University, London.

———. *Women and War*. 1915. Reprint. New York: Garland Press, 1972.

Taylor, A. J. P. *English History: 1914–1945*. London: Oxford University Press, 1965.

———. *The Trouble Makers: Dissent over Foreign Policy 1792–1939*. London: Hamish Hamilton, 1967.

Taylor, Eric. *Women Who Went to War*. London: Robert Hale, 1988.

Theweleit, Klaus. *Male Fantasies*. 2 vols. Minneapolis: University of Minnesota Press, 1987.

The Times Guide to the House of Commons. London: Times Books. 1992 (published after each U.K. general election.)

Tylee, Claire M. *The Great War and Women's Consciousness*. Iowa City: University of Iowa Press, 1990.

———. "Maleness Run Riot—The Great War and Women's Resistance to Militarism." In *Women's Studies International Forum* 11: 3 (1988).

Vallance, Elizabeth. *Women in the House*. London: The Athlone Press, 1979.

Vassiltchikov, Marie. *The Berlin Diaries 1940–1945*. London: Methuen, 1987.

Wadge, D. Collett. *Women in Uniform*. London: Sampson Low, Marston & Co. Ltd., 1946.

War Office Statistics. His Majesty's Stationery Office, 1919.

White, Cynthia. *Women's Magazines 1693–1968*, London: Michael Joseph, 1970.

Wiltsher, Anne. *Most Dangerous Women*. London: Pandora Press, 1985.

Wolf, Christa. *A Model Childhood*. (Kindheitmuster) Tr. Ursule Molinaro and Hedwig Rappolt. London: Virago, 1983.

———. *The Quest for Christa T.* Tr. Christopher Middleton. London: Virago, 1982.

Woman Today. British Library Periodical Holdings, Colindale, London.

Women's Studies Quarterly 12:2 (1984): 13–15. British Library Periodical Holdings, Colindale, London.

Woolf, Virginia. *The Death of the Moth and Other Essays.* Harmondsworth: Penguin Books, 1961.

———. *Three Guineas.* New York: Harcourt, Brace & Company, 1938.

Index

Abdela, Lesley, 79
Ackland, Valentine, "7 October, 1940," 156
Addams, Jane, 32, 33, 80
Air Force, Equipment Units, 111
Air Raid Precautions (ARP), 110, 125
Akhmatova, Anna: "July 1914," 48
Allan, Mabel Esther, 160
Allied governments, 81
American Association of University Women, 87
Anderson, Mary, 71
appeasement, 78, 105
Armed Forces, British, 111
armed services, women in, 110
Army Transfusion Service, 111
Asquith, Herbert H., 28, 36, 39, 88
Associated governments, 81
Astor, David, 136
Astor, Lady, 76
Atholl, Duchess of, 78, 106
Auden, W. H., 146
Augspurg, Anita, 31, 88, 92
Auxiliary Territorial Service (ATS), 111, 117, 142, 159
Axmann, Artur, 96
Ayers, Pat, 119–20

Baer, Gertrude, 81, 93, 99, 108
Bagnold, Enid, 60
Balch, Emily Greene, 32, 80, 81
Baldwin, Lord, 23
Balfour, Arthur James, 28
Banerjee, A., 141
Bates, Rachel, 170
Battle of Britain, 120. See also Blitz, of London
Bäumer, Gertrud, 31, 88, 98
Bax, Vera, 155; "The Fallen," 154; "To Billy, My Son," 154; "To Richard, My Son," 153

Bebel, August: Women Under Socialism, 91
Bedford, Ida, 176; "Munitions Wages," 64
Bellerby, Frances: "War Casualty in April," 148
Bergonzi, Bernard, 42
Berlin, bombing of, 124, 125, 128, 129, 167
Berry, Paul, 107, 130
Bevin, Ernest, 118
Bielenberg, Christabel, 128, 137; The Past Is Myself, 127
Bishop, Alan, 107, 130
blackout, 112
Blitz, of London, 120, 121, 122, 159, 164, 167
Blunden, Edmund, 42, 49; "Third Ypres," 48, 52
Boileau, Winifred: "Sounds," 159
Bondfield, Margaret, 105
Bottomley, Virginia, 79
Bridges, Robert, 42
Britannia, 27, 29. See also The Suffragette
British Committee Against War and Fascism, 84
British Expeditionary Force (BEF), 116
Brittain, Vera, 43, 59, 69, 103, 107, 108–9, 124, 125, 129, 135; "Lament for Cologne," 122, 123; Seed of Chaos, 122, 123, 130; Testament of a Generation, 130
Brooke, Rupert, 141
Brookes, Pamela, 106, 118
Bund Deutscher Frauenvereine (BDF), 31, 88, 98
Bund Deutscher Mädchen (BDM), 96
Bussey, Gertrude, 32, 81, 82, 83, 92, 93, 108
Butler, Rupert, 96

Caen, battle of, 96
Cavell, Edith, 60
Chamberlain, Neville, 78, 101, 102
Charman, T. C., 37
children, 161, 163–64
Christianity, 56, 60, 70, 71
Church of England, 57, 72
Churchill, Winston, 78, 108, 116, 117, 121, 129, 137–38
Clark, Lois, 164–65
Coats, Alice: "Sky-Conscious," 165
Cole, Margaret Postgate, 69; "Afterwards," 67, 68
Coleman, Marion, 148–49
Collier, Richard, 116, 120
Colville, John, 136, 137
Comfort, Alix, 143
Committee for Peace in Spain, 86
communism, 103, 105; German, 136
concentration camps, 162
conscientious objection, 37, 111
conscription, of women, 111, 113, 118, 119, 120
Co-operative Guild, 107
Cornford, Frances: "Casualties," 168
Costello, John, 115
Coulson, Leslie: "Who Made the Law?" 53–54
Courtney, Kate, 25, 28, 34–35, 54, 132
Cromer, Lord, 28

death, as poetic theme, 153, 157–61
De Bairacli-Levy, Juliette, 170
Depression of 1930s, 106
Despard, Mrs. Charlotte, 74
disarmament, 82, 83, 101
Dobell, Eva, 44; "Night Duty," 58; "Pluck," 59
Dobell, Mrs. C. Oliver: "Son of Mine," 61
Douglas, Keith, 140–41, 144, 146, 150–51, 156, 157, 158, 176; "Cairo Jag," 152; "Elegy for an 88 Gunner," 167–68; "How to Kill," 168; "Simplify Me When I'm Dead," 157–58
Dunkirk, 116–17

East End Settlement, 38
Eden, Anthony, 116
Eliot, T. S.: *The Waste Land*, 151
Elshtain, Jean Bethke, 38

Emancipation Act of 7 December 1917, 75
employment, of women, 23, 24, 77, 88, 175
enfranchisement of women, in Germany, 100
evacuation, 112–13
Evans, Dorothy, 84

Falklands War, 173
family, 43, 113, 161
Farjeon, Eleanor: "Peace," 72–73
Fasci Feminili, 86
fascism, 92, 94, 99, 100, 101, 103, 109
Fawcett, Henry, 40
Fawcett, Millicent, 25, 27, 28, 29, 31, 88
Fellowship for Reconciliation, 37
feminism, 92, 94; militant, 75, 95
feminists, 91, 94, 173
"Flapper Election" (Election of 1929), 77
Ford, S. Gertrude: "A Fight to a Finish," 63–64; "The Tenth Armistice Day," 64, 72
Frauenschaft, 93
Frauenwerk, 97
"Freedom" Radio Station, 100
Freud, Sigmund, 43, 133
front-line experience, 46–50. See also home front
Fuller, Roy, 144
Fussell, Paul, 42, 49, 54, 130

Gardner, Brian, 141, 144, 145
Gellhorn, Martha, 135
general election, 1918, 74–75
German peace women activists, 92
German resistance to Hitler, 136
Gershon, Karen: "Home," 162; "A Jew's Calendar," 162
Gilbert, Sandra M., 43, 44
Gort, Lord, 116
Graves, Robert, 43, 141, 142, 146
Griffiths, Grace: "Doodlebugs," 159–60
Gubar, Susan, 43, 44
Gulf War, 173

Hallgarten, Constanze, 92
Hamilton, Cicely: "Non-Combatant," 44

Harris, Arthur, 126, 129
Harrison, Brian, 25, 28
Hastings, Max, 129
Henderson, Mary, 44; "An Incident," 56
Hermann, Liselotte ("Lilo"), 90, 99
Hewison, Robert, 143, 144
Heymann, Lida Gustava, 31, 80, 88, 92
Higonnet, Margaret R., 43, 44, 106
Hill, W. T., 60
Himmler, Heinrich, 97
Hitler, Adolph, 93, 95, 97, 99, 100, 103, 109, 127, 129, 132, 136, 137; assassination attempt, see July 1944 plot
Hitler Jugend (HJ), 95, 96, 97
Hitler Youth. See Hitler Jugend
Hobhouse, Emily, 25, 28, 29, 30, 33, 38, 46, 73, 132
Holmes, Pamela: "Missing, Presumed Killed," 155; "War Baby," 161
Holtby, Winifred, 84
home front, 42, 43, 44, 50, 51, 133, 144
Home Guard, 133
Horsbrugh, Florence, 105
Hughes, Ted, 158
humanism, 108
Hunkins-Hall, Hazel, 84
Huxley, Julian, 132

international feminism, 108
international socialism, 91
International Suffrage Alliance, 32
International Suffrage Peace Association, 27
international women, 85–93
International Women's Peace Conference (April-May 1915), 25, 27, 28, 31, 32, 33, 35, 61, 80, 92, 104
International Women's Suffrage Alliance, 30
internationalism, 79, 94, 108
Irons, Evelyn, 114, 115
Italy, 86; women's enfranchisement in, 87

Jackson, Ada: "Blessed Event," 157
Jacobs, Aletta, 32
Jarman, Wrenne: "It Happened Before," 169–70; "Threnody for Berlin—1945," 167

Jesse, F. Tennyson: "Note to Isolationists, 1940," 142–43
jingoism, 25, 28, 29, 62, 63
Jones, Cecilia: "Shipbound," 160
Juchaczo, Marie, 91
July 1944 plot, 136, 137
Jus Suffragii, 63, 80

Kahn, Nosheen, 43, 45, 50
Keilhau, Frau, 34
Kellogg Pact, 83
Key, Ellen, 30–31
Keyes, Sidney, 141, 144, 156, 157, 158; "The Wilderness," 151
Keys, Evelyn, 73
Kirkpatrick, Clifford, 89, 90, 93, 97
Kollwitz, Käthe, 59, 155
Koonz, Claudia, 95, 97, 98; Mothers in the Fatherland, 94

Labour Party, 94
Last, Nella, 131–32
Lawrence, Mrs. Pethick, 74
League of German Women's Associations, 88
League of Mothers and Educators for Peace, 86
League of Nations, 37, 78, 80, 81, 82, 83, 87, 93, 105, 109
Lebensborn, 96
Ledward, Patricia, 145, 169, 176
Leibknecht, Karl, 90
Lewis, Alun, 141, 142, 144, 157, 158, 176; "Burma Casualty," 146–47; "The Mahratta Ghats," 150–51
Lewis, Jane, 114, 119
Liddington, Jane, 107, 109
Lindsay, Olive: "Despair," 67
Lusitania, sinking of, 36
Luxemburg, Rosa, 90

Macaulay, Rose, 51, 57, 141, 176; "Picnic," 45, 46, 47, 50; "The Shadow," 50, 51, 53
MacKenzie, Mrs. H. M., 74
Macmillan, Chrystal, 28, 32
MacNeice, Louis, 146
magazines and newspapers, British women's, 85
Major, John, 79, 80
Mannin, Ethel: "Song of the Bomber," 165–66

Markiewicz, Countess, 75
marriage, in Germany, 90
Marshall, Catherine, 25, 30, 54, 74, 85
"masculine principle," 97
maternity, 156
McKenna, Reginald, 26
Mead, Margaret, 135
Mew, Charlotte, 71, 176; "The Cenotaph," 70; "May 1915," 48
Meynell, Alice, 52, 57, 60; "Summer in England, 1914," 51–52, 53
milicianas, 86
militancy, female, 133
militants, 39
militarism, 25, 27, 28, 30, 32, 40, 57, 73, 112, 135, 175
militarization, of women, 112
Mill, John Stuart, 40
Ministry of Home Security, 116
Ministry of Information, 116
Minns, Raynes, 122
Mitchell, David, 37, 60, 64
Mitchell, Ruth Comfort: "He Went for a Soldier," 55, 57
Modern Woman, 107
Moore, Henry, 121
Moorehead, Caroline, 62
Morgan, David, 26, 27, 40
Morrison, Sybil, 84
munitions factories, 114
munitions workers, 64
Mussolini, Benito, 103, 137

National Committee of Jewish Women, 87
National Committee on the Cause and the Cure of War (U.S.), 87
National Council of Women, 110
National Federation of Women's Institutes, 110
National Peace Council, 107
national service, 111
National Service Act, 111
National Service Act (No. 2), 118
National Union of Townswomen's Guilds, 110
National Union of Women's Suffrage Societies (NUWSS), 25, 27, 28, 30, 31, 88
nationalism, 25, 28, 88, 175
nationalist feminists, 89

National Women's Service. *See* Bund Deutscher Frauenvereine
nature imagery, in poetry, 147, 148, 150, 156
Nazi party, 94, 95, 97, 98, 100, 128, 134, 136
Nazism, 99, 109
Nazi youth, 133. *See also* Hitler Jugend
Neo-Georgians, 146
Newberry, Jo Vellacott, 30
Non-Conscription League, 37
nonresistance, 82
NSDAP, 94
nurses, World War I. *See* Voluntary Aid Detachments

Oldfield, Sybil, 54, 133, 137; *Women Against the Iron Fist*, 132
Orwell, George, 130
Owen, Wilfred, 42, 48, 49, 56, 69, 71, 140, 141, 172, 176; "À Terre," 58–59; "Anthem for a Dead Youth," 63; "Anthem for Doomed Youth," 71; "Dulce et Decorum Est," 57, 63; "Futility," 54; "Miners," 68; "Sensibility," 47; "Strange Meeting," 54, 168

pacifism, 30, 31, 32, 36, 37, 61, 83, 94, 101, 103, 109, 143
pacifists, 34, 37, 39, 69, 80, 85, 88, 92, 102, 107, 130, 133, 154, 173; feminists, 89, 109; women writers, 103
Pankhurst, Christabel, 24, 25, 27, 28, 29, 38, 39, 73, 75
Pankhurst, Emmeline, 23, 24, 25, 26, 27, 28, 29, 31, 38, 39, 73, 88
Pankhurst, Sylvia, 25, 26, 27, 28, 29, 38, 39, 73
Park, Alice, 33
Parliament, women in, 74, 79, 105, 147, 174
patriotism, 25, 88
Pax International, 107
Peace and Disarmament Committee of the Women's International Organization, 86, 87, 101
Peace Committee of the International Council of Women, 87
Peace Pledge Union, 107, 109
Philipson, Mrs. Hilton, 76

pieta image, 59, 60, 61
Pinkard, Bertram, 109
political candidates, women as, 74
Pope, Jessie, 29, 63; "The Call," 62
popular front, 105
Pore, Renata, 92
precision bombing, 122, 124
Price, Nancy, 168
protest poems, 53, 54
psychological trauma, 43, 58
psychology of war, 133

Queen Alexandra's Imperial Military Nursing Service (QAIMNS), 160
Queen Mary's Army Auxiliary Corps, 45

Ramelson, Maria, 26, 29, 37
Rathbone, Eleanor, 104, 105; War Can Be Averted, 78, 105
Read, Sir Herbert Edward, 42
Read, Sylvia: "For the War-Children," 164
Red Cross, 88
Reichsschrifttumskammer, 134
Reichstag, 92, 104; women in, 89
Reilly, Catherine, 42, 44, 48, 62, 73, 140, 145, 147
religion, 57, 155; symbols of, 151, 166, 167
Rempel, Gerhard, 95, 97
Representation of the People act and bill, 39, 40
resistance movement, in Germany, 136, 137
Rhondda, Viscountess, 83
Ridler, Anne, 143, 145; "Now as Then," 143
Rilke, Ranier Maria, 158
Ritchie, J. M., 134
Robins, Elizabeth, 84
Rolland, Romain, 85
Roosevelt, Eleanor, 101, 102
Roosevelt, Franklin D., 137
Rosenberg, Isaac, 42, 49, 141
Rover, Constance, 25, 40
Royal Air Force (RAF), 117
Royal Observer Corps, 118
Royden, Maude, 56, 108, 109, 132, 164
Rupp, Leila, 92, 98, 99
Russell, Bertrand, 109
Russell, Dora, 84

Sassoon, Siegfried, 42, 47, 49, 56, 69, 71, 176; "Aftermath," 48; "Base Details," 66, 70; Counter-Attack, 49, 67; "Glory of Women," 67; "Suicide in the Trenches," 66, 67; "They," 57, 59; "Wirers," 63; "Working Party," 63
Sayers, Dorothy: "The English War," 143
Scannell, Vernon, 142
Scholl, Hans, 137
Scholl, Sophie, 137
Scholtz-Klink, Gertrud, 95, 97, 98
Schreiner, Olive, 25, 28, 30; Woman and Labour, 33, 105
Schwimmer, Rosika, 32
Searchlight Batteries, 111
Selwyn, Victor, 145
sentimentality, 147
separate spheres, 98
Sewall, May Wright, 33, 55
Sex Disqualification Removal Act, 114
Sharp, Evelyn, 35, 36
Sheepshanks, Mary, 63
Shephard, Gillian, 79
Sheppard, Dick, 109
Sheridan, Dorothy, 110, 112, 113
Silkin, John, 48
Sinclair, May, 44, 141; "Field Ambulance in Retreat," 57–58
Sitwell, Edith, 66, 145, 176; "The Dancers," 65, 66; "Still Falls the Rain," 48, 145, 166
Six Point Group, 83–84, 115
Smith, Constance Babington, 112
Smith, Harry, 116
socialism, 91, 92
soldier poets, 42, 45, 48, 49, 50, 52, 59, 66, 71, 72, 161
Somme, Battle of the, 141
Sorley, Charles, 71
Sozialdemokratische Partei Deutschlands (SPD), 89
Spain, women's movmement, 85
Spanish civil war, 86
Special Operations Executive (SOE), 111
Spender, Stephen, 141, 146
Stafford, Jean, 85, 101, 102
Stafford, Sarah: "The Unborn," 156
Stalin, Joseph, 103

Stephenson, Jill, 92
Strachey, Ray, 26, 27, 39
Strang, Colin, 145
suffrage movement, 23, 40, 74, 91, 173
suffrage societies, 38, 39
suffrage, women's, 24, 25, 39, 55, 56, 88, 104
Suffragette, The, 24, 26, 27, 29, 37. See also *Britannia*
suffragists, 23, 42, 64, 74, 75, 88; antimilitant, 27; antiwar, 25, 27, 29, 53; militant, 23, 28, 29, 40, 74, 75; pacifist, 35, 37, 38, 40, 74; prowar, 25, 34
Summerskill, Edith, 118, 133
Swanwick, Helena, 25, 28, 29, 30, 34, 35, 39, 40, 61, 74, 80, 85, 103, 108, 132, 154; *I Have Been Young*, 83

Taylor, A. J. P., 141
Teasdale, Sara, "Spring in War-Time," 67
Thatcher, Margaret, 79
Thomas, Edward, 141
300 Group for Women in Politics and Public Life, 79
Tims, Margaret, 32, 81, 82, 83, 92, 93, 108
trade unionists, 90
Tree, Iris, 60
trench warfare, 43, 46, 48, 54, 68, 148
Tylee, Claire, 141

unconditional surrender, 128, 137
United Nations, 107

Vassiltchikov, Marie ("Missie"), 124, 127, 128, 129, 137; *Berlin Diaries*, 126
Vatican, 137
Versailles, Treaty of, 81, 82, 128
Vietnam War, 173
violence, male and female, 38
Voluntary Aid Detachments (VAD), 44, 56, 57, 59, 60
Von Bismarck-Schönhausen, Gottfried, 137
Von Haeften, Hans-Bertrand, 137
Von Helldorf, Count Wolf-Heinrich, 137
Von Hohenlohe, Prince Max, 136, 137
Von Schirach, Baldur, 95, 96

Von Stauffenberg, Count Claus Schenck, 137
Von Suttner, Bertha, 135, 136
Von Trott zu Solz, Adam, 137

Wadge, Collett, 45
Wainwright, Margaret, 171
Ward, Irene, 118
Ward, Mrs. Alexander, 29
Warner, Sylvia Townsend, 176; "Road 1940," 163, 164
War Office, 116
War Office Signal Office, 111
wartime pacifists, 27
Watson, Mrs. Chalmers, 45
Weimar constitution, 89
Wellesley, Dorothy: "Spring in the Park (London: 1919–1943)," 149–50
Whateley, Monica, 84
white-feather campaign, 29
white-feather poetry, 62
White Rose, 137
Wilkinson, Ellen, 78, 104, 105
Wilson, Marjorie, 72
Wilson, Woodrow, 81, 83
Wiltsher, Anne, 31, 32
Wintringham, Mrs., 76
Wintringham, Tom, 76
Wolf, Christa, 134; *Kindheitmuster (A Model Childhood)*, 133; *The Quest for Christa T.*, 134–35
Woman Suffrage Campaign, 23
Woman's Daily, 85
Woman's National Newspaper, 85
Woman's Newspaper, 85, 101
Woman Today, 85, 86, 98, 99, 100
women pacifist writers, 131
Women's Army Auxiliary Corps (WAACs), 45
Women's Auxiliary Air Force (WAAF), 111, 112, 117, 142
Women's Christian Temperance Union, 87
Women's Consultative Committee, 118
women's emancipation, 25
Women's Engineering Society, 115
Women's Freedom League, 84
Women's Home Defence, 133
Women's Independent Party, 74

Women's International League for Peace and Freedom (WILPF), 36, 38, 80, 81, 82, 83, 87, 92, 93, 103, 107, 108; in Germany, 92, 99; in the United States, 102
Women's Land Army, 118, 119
Women's League of Unity, 85, 101, 102, 103
women's movement, in Germany, 88, 93
Women's Party, 39, 74, 75
Women's Peace Conference. See International Women's Peace Conference
Women's Royal Naval Service (WRNS), 111, 117, 142
Women's Social and Political Union, 24, 25, 26, 28, 31, 88

Women's Suffrage and Political Union, 75
Women's Suffrage League, 31, 88
Women's Voluntary Service (WVS), 122
Women's World Committee Against War and Fascism, 84, 85
Woolf, Leonard, 116, 131
Woolf, Virginia, 103, 109, 116, 130, 131, 133; Between the Acts, 133; Three Guineas, 132
workforce, women in, 113, 117
World Peace Congress, 85
Wyse, Elizabeth: "Auschwitz," 171

Zetkin, Clara, 90